PLAYING
SMART

TRANSFORM YOUR GOLF
WITHOUT CHANGING
YOUR SWING

DAVID RICHARDS

Matador
9 Priory Business Park,
Wistow Road, Kibworth Beauchamp,
Leicestershire. LE8 0RX
Tel: (+44) 116 279 2299
Fax: (+44) 116 279 2277
Email: books@troubador.co.uk
Web: www.troubador.co.uk/matador

ISBN 978-1784620-486

British Library Cataloguing in Publication Data.
A catalogue record for this book is available from the British Library.

Typeset in 12pt Adobe Devanagari by Troubador Publishing Ltd, Leicester, UK
Printed and bound in the UK by TJ International, Padstow, Cornwall

Matador is an imprint of Troubador Publishing Ltd

I would like to thank the many golfers I have played golf with over the last 20 years who have inspired me to write this book. I have learned much by witnessing all manner of problems and observing smart play in its many forms.

I would also like to thank the people who encouraged me to write the book. I am particularly grateful to those who spent their time reading drafts and providing constructive comments. You know who you are and I thank you all.

CONTENTS

FOREWORD by BARNEY PUTTICK

SENIOR GOLF PROFESSIONAL AND FELLOW OF THE PGA

Over the years I've taught many people, from beginners to the elite golfers. In common with other teaching professionals, my typical clients mainly want to work on their full swings. Second to this come technical aspects of the short game, especially putting.

But very few ask about game management. This is despite the fact that 'thinking your way around the golf course' will for many be an obvious and immediate way of improving their scores.

I met David some years ago when he came to me for some help with his swing. During our sessions it struck me how knowledgeable he is about golf in general. He is what I would describe as 'an observational golfer', with an open and enquiring mind. He has witnessed literally thousands of rounds played by all manner of regular golfers, so he really understands the challenges that they face.

I was intrigued when he mentioned one day that he had started writing about golf, in particular about the non-swing related aspects that helped him to get his handicap down to single figures.

When he produced the manuscript I was immediately taken with it. I am well read on the subject of golf but cannot think of any other book that addresses the principles of good course and game management to this extent. It is obvious that many golfers could benefit from this.

He has managed to cover 'the fundamentals of good golf' in a practical and clear way, focusing on sound principles, whilst not being too prescriptive. The book also explains how to assess non swing-related weaknesses in the long and short game, and gives sound suggestions about how to go about improvement.

One thing that comes through in the book is that David really knows his subject. Traditional golf book authors tend to be golf coaches who spend the majority of their time at the driving range. Compared to this, he has far more experience of the problems that average golfers face on the course.

David also has a way of bringing out the key points that make the most difference to a golfer's play. It is clear that he has an analytical and insightful mind.

I was delighted when he asked me to write a foreword for this book, and I'm only too pleased to do so. I have no doubt that the vast majority of golfers will, in some way, find this a useful read. And I fully expect many to get their handicaps down as a result.

Barney Puttick
Senior Golf Professional
Fellow of the PGA

INTRODUCTION

The game of golf is captivating. Once you are taken in there is no escape. It offers the promise of great rounds, fantastic shots, pressure-putts and glorious victories. But it also frustrates in equal measure. It's in the nature of the game that, on average, our scores and individual shots are never quite what we want them to be.

This creates the desire to improve. Or at an absolute minimum to maintain our current standard of play, and certainly to arrest any possible decline. Hence a good proportion of golfers can be seen at the driving range. The default response to the desire to improve seems to be to hit more balls in the hope of grooving a better swing.

Other golfers frequently change their equipment in the belief that they will play better. The golf industry's product marketing machine is formidable. It gives us hope that there is a longer and more forgiving driver or set of irons out there; we just need to buy them.

Some players look for expertise and turn to golf professionals for help. Typical requests are to *improve my swing, be more consistent, stop slicing* or *get more distance*. Many try self-improvement and read books, watch DVDs or study video clips.

Serious players know that the short game and putting are where a good proportion of shots are lost and gained. They can be seen practising, chipping from the fringe, or stroking putts to and from the flags on the practice putting green.

These approaches can help, but improvements are often short-lived, or there comes a point where progress halts. More practice, lessons, new equipment or reading has no further effect. A natural limit is reached based on the golfer's fundamental ability to strike the ball, and chip and putt.

Yet amongst players of the same raw ability, some repeatedly out-perform others. These golfers consistently score better than the quality of their ball striking, the accuracy of their short games, and their putting skills. How can this be? What is it that they do or know that others don't?

These golfers are *playing smart*. They make better decisions and fewer mistakes than those with similar skills. They assess the challenge of each shot rationally and reach sound conclusions. They prepare well and do everything possible to ensure a good outcome. They use their minds to get ahead.

Little has been written about this. The majority of self-help books concentrate on the full swing. 'How to use your existing skills to score better' is generally only mentioned as an afterthought, if at all. Yet nearly every golfer I know wants to *do the best he can with what he's got*.

I wrote this book to fill this gap. In every area of the game I describe a set of principles that 'smart golfers' repeatedly use to get the edge over other players. I also explain how a golfer might analyse his game to properly identify the non-swing related problems that repeatedly cost shots.

The book is suitable for the vast majority of golfers. If you are a competent player, it should help you to score better. If you already play to a good standard, it should provide a means to highlight where you still have room for improvement. If you are a beginner, then you could stand to gain even more.

Incorporating the principles in this book should help to accelerate your journey to better golf, whatever your starting point.

At a minimum, this book provides a checklist of 'good practice'. At a maximum, the approaches suggested could make a real difference to your ability to score well.

I hope it will provide you with a means to transform your game. Read on and let's see.

OVERVIEW – THE SMART GOLFER

On the tee the smart golfer considers the angles and finds a good spot to play from. He works out the best line of play and appreciates that a drive is 'just another layup'. He also makes a point of aiming well.

When playing from the fairway or from the first cut of rough he routinely examines lies and slopes. He knows that these can restrict what is possible, reduce accuracy, and might require a modified shot or change of target.

When the smart golfer needs to compromise, he does so unhesitatingly. He has a favourite layup distance from which he is usually very accurate, not least because he practises this yardage as a matter of course.

He calculates distances easily and well, allowing for wind and elevation. He knows how far he hits the ball with each club in his bag and is realistic about this. His well-struck approach shots are therefore nearly always 'pin-high' or thereabouts. He also consistently makes the right club and shot selections when playing to uphill and downhill greens.

The smart golfer appreciates that from 100 yards and in, being able to hit the ball the right distance is critical to good scoring. He is able to adjust the length of his shots within 'scoring range', using a three-quarter-length swing with adjustments.

He knows the strength and direction of the wind, and understands the impact of this on ball flight. His three-quarter shot helps him to be more accurate on windy days – these shots have less spin, and penetrate the wind and hold their line better.

The smart golfer makes sure that he has a precise target and aim-line, and is clear that these are two different things. He makes every effort to align properly at address. He appreciates that a poor setup often produces a poor result, and that good posture is also important.

He repeatedly sets up well to maximise his chances of success. By being consistent, he is able to better diagnose a problem because he knows that his 'fundamentals' are good.

The smart golfer plots his way around the course, aiming for the wide areas of the fairway and the centre of greens. He is aware of the importance of 'local knowledge', understands the terrain of his local course, and will have looked at the holes 'back to front'.

He understands that course designers set out to trick golfers with 'illusions'. He works out the best angles to play into greens. He plays to his strengths, works around his weaknesses, and gets the most out of his approach play.

Good decision-making is at the heart of good golf. The smart golfer knows how to weigh up a marginal shot and appreciates the importance of understanding both the chances of success and the consequences of failure.

He usually keeps his ball comfortably in play and rarely plays a shot without a sound rationale. But if there is a good reason to go-for-it, he won't hesitate. If his shot then doesn't work out, he takes the pain in his stride, and moves on undeterred.

A smart golfer excels at handling trouble and avoids compound errors. He appreciates that a good recovery shot requires the consideration of distance, as well as line. He makes a point of always using the optimum club.

He is an expert at finding his ball, not through luck, but by the application of skill and good judgement. If there is a possibility that his ball might be lost, he always plays 'a provisional'. He is good at this because it is routine to him.

The smart golfer consistently clears the lips of fairway bunkers and doesn't hesitate to play a splash shot if there is a problem. He has good skills to escape from the trees and has mastered the 'low shot' to make this easier.

He handles the rough well, using good technique. If there is any doubt about cleanly getting out first time, he considers other options including a 'drop' and playing a different line.

The smart golfer has a sense of being largely in control of his long game. Even when he is striking the ball poorly, he still manages to do quite well. He consistently gets from tee to green efficiently, and rarely wastes a shot.

He systematically assesses his performance and separates outcomes from factors in his control. He is clear on the difference between a mental error (relating to decision-making and preparation) and a physical error (caused by a poor setup or swing). By understanding his play from all angles he is easily able to work on the things that matter most.

The smart golfer appreciates that a good short game makes all the difference to his score.

He understands that most golfers' pitch shots are fairly straight, but that distance control is a major problem. He therefore focuses on this, both on the course and during practice.

He always aims at a precise landing spot. He also seeks to leave the ball below the hole, and away from the short-side. When the situation requires something different, he is competent at both 'pitch and run' and lob shots.

The smart golfer has a sound chipping technique. He increases his accuracy by keeping the ball low, thereby minimising unhelpful bounce effects. He is also aware that 'touch' is important in the short game. To ensure consistency he always uses the same make and type of ball.

Since many chips are from slopes or longer grass, he regularly practises from these lies. He is at least adequate with greenside bunker play and rarely fails to get out first time. He also makes sound shot choices around the green, for example when he's 'short-sided'.

Golfers can play exceptionally well from tee to green but still walk off with a high score if they don't putt well. The smart golfer appreciates that good putters nearly always have a good putting stroke, since it is much easier to get the ball into the hole with sound technique.

He understands that a good 'roll' is all-important, watches for this, and knows how to assess his putting stroke. If he has a problem with any putting fundamentals, he will work on these and won't hesitate to seek assistance if required.

The smart golfer appreciates that 'pace is everything' on the green. He understands that, provided he gets this right, he will hole a good share of putts no matter what. He also knows that poor pace on a long putt is often *the* reason for a three-putt, so he regularly practises this length.

In order to have the best possible information on the pace required, he walks the length of the putt, assesses the speed of the surface, and notes the extent to which the hole is up or downhill.

The smart golfer has a routine for reading and executing putts. This creates consistency. He is calm and relaxed over the ball, and makes sure that he gives even the shortest of putts great respect.

He understands how important it is to have a positive attitude towards putting and appreciates that even the best putts sometimes don't go in. He is able to diagnose his putting problems. He works out if a bad putt is a result of a poor read, poor alignment, or the stroke itself.

The smart golfer practises in proportion and focuses on the problems that cost him the most shots. He divides his time equally between the Long Game, the Short Game and Putting in the ratio 1/3, 1/3, 1/3.

He is well prepared before leaving home to play. He arrives relaxed and in plenty of time, thereby avoiding unnecessary stress. He will also have decided on his objectives for the day, including whether to be generally aggressive or conservative. He thinks through, in advance, whether to warm up or not and is relaxed about this.

The smart golfer always spends ten minutes on the practice green before play – he knows that it doesn't make sense for his first putt or chip of the day to be out on the course. He also has a clear plan for this precious time, and uses it to best effect.

He has learned to make his first shot of the day 'routine' and sets himself reasonable expectations. During his round everything he does appears to be matter of fact. He has a good pre-shot routine, which flows well and he rarely suffers from time pressure.

The smart golfer understands the effect of being tired. He knows that if he is mentally below his best, his game will suffer. During a round he stays hydrated and appreciates that it makes sense to keep his energy levels topped up.

Importantly, he adopts a rational attitude both on and off the course. When judging his round he separates how well he played, from the score or result. He accepts that luck is even-handed.

The smart golfer has an above average knowledge of the rules that matter, and legitimately uses these to his advantage. He embraces the spirit of golf and is a pillar of integrity and consideration for others.

His focus on enjoyment helps him feel more content whatever the day has thrown at him – he maintains a positive attitude. Irrespective of the standard of his golf, he is well prepared, works within his abilities, uses his head, and feels on top of his game.

NOTE TO READERS

In the book I have assumed that the reader is a right-handed golfer. Clearly a proportion of players are 'lefties'. But in order to avoid lengthy explanations, and to simplify things, my descriptions have been made from the point of view of a right-handed golfer. For example when I mention a 'fade' I assume a shape from left to right.

Similarly, a good proportion of players are lady golfers. Once again I have sought to simplify things and maintain the flow of the text by using the male gender throughout. For example I use 'he', and not 'he/she'. Nevertheless, please be assured that this book is of equal relevance to all golfers alike.

GROUND MATTERS

The tee provides several opportunities for the 'thinking golfer' at the start of each hole. Elsewhere on the course the choice of shot is constrained by the condition of the ground, the lie of the ball, and the slopes affecting the stance and swing.

1.   ON THE TEE

A smart golfer takes the opportunity to position the ball on the tee, finds the best place for the shot, and makes sure he aims well.

The tee is the only place on the course where you can choose where you place your ball and be assured of a great lie, by using a tee peg. The smart golfer picks a spot so that he is on good ground and has a solid base for his swing. He also uses the space available to get the best angle for the shot.

Many players just stroll up to the centre of the tee and put a tee peg in without a moment's thought. Others always set up on the right (or left) side, or merely place the ball down near the spot that the previous player played from. In contrast, the smart golfer makes a conscious choice to position his ball. He works out if one side or the other offers him some advantage by improving the line of play.

For example, with water on the right hand side of a hole, but no real problems to the left, smart golfers will typically play from the right side of the tee. This is because the aim-line from here to the centre of the fairway is more 'away' from the water than if the ball were teed up on the far left.

Another example might be on a hole with trees running from the tee close down the left hand side towards the hole. In this instance our smart golfer might also choose to tee up on the right hand side because this reduces any sense that the trees are 'encroaching' into the shot (also playing from the right might decrease the chances of hitting a protruding branch in flight).

The equation for golfers with an institutional shot-shape (such as a regular fade, draw, slice or hook) will be different to those whose ball flight is predominantly straight. With a curved shape, the ball moves in one direction at take-off, and another at landing and as it rolls out.

Deciding which side of the tee to play from has both a rational component – *which line of play gives me the best chance to avoid trouble or gain advantage?* – and an emotional one – *which side of the tee do I feel most comfortable with?* Both of these elements are important but the latter is critical. Any discomfort over the ball can translate into body tension, which in turn can produce a poor swing.

In summary, choose the side of the tee that gives you the best chance of hitting the fairway, whilst avoiding any major problems, and feeling as relaxed as possible over the ball.

On some courses the tees are well worn, often in a line near the markers, with scuffmarks and divot holes that can affect your footing. The smart golfer tries to take his stance on good ground. If this isn't possible between the markers, he will place his ball several feet back (noting the need to be within two club lengths of the front line). He knows that it is more important to have good footing and a clean area to play from, than it is to gain an extra yard or so.

Whilst choosing his spot, the smart golfer might also get some help with his alignment. After working out the shot he wants to play, he thinks about lining up. A good way to do this is to place the ball so that it forms a straight line between the target and a mark on the tee (such as a scuff or old divot hole).

As the player moves in to address the shot, he sets up square to the line formed by the ball and the divot/scuffmark. He is therefore now certain that he is lined up with his target.

I will discuss the importance of good aim in more depth later. But whilst we are 'on the tee' I would like to touch on a particular problem in relation to 'dogleg' holes (holes with a sharp left or right turn). On these holes, some players are seduced to play in the direction of the flag (trying to cut the corner too much). Others are aware of this problem and sometimes over-compensate away from the corner, aiming too far out/wide, particularly if there is severe trouble on the other side.

Having setup on the wrong line, it is not unusual for a golfer to sense that they are misaligned and automatically compensate during the swing (often with an interesting 'contortion' followed by a poor result). So if sometimes you wonder why your swing or shot outcome was unusually poor for no apparent reason on a dogleg hole, consider if this might be the reason.

The key thing to fix in your mind is that the target is the centre of the fairway. Once you are clear on this avoid all thoughts about the pin, or about shying away from trouble.

Over time, positioning the ball on the tee comes automatically to the smart golfer. On each hole at his home course he will have worked out the best side to play from, noting that this can differ for different tee boxes on the same hole if these are set at different angles to the fairway.

Uphill and downhill shots from the tee can create an altogether different type of problem. The visual effect of a hole that slopes uphill can translate into a desire to hit the ball harder than usual. Similarly, the sight of a downhill hole can also prompt a harder swing, with the player perhaps imagining a 'career-best' drive.

These factors don't seduce the smart golfer – he knows that it is a priority to leave the ball 'on the short stuff' and to not end up in trouble. The negative effect of being straight but 20 or 30 yards short of your best driver-distance, is far less than the negative effect of being offline if the ball ends up in the rough, trees or a fairway bunker.

Many average golfers persist in thinking that it is necessary, indeed mandatory, to give each drive 'all they've got'. But it isn't. The best golfers rarely try to 'come out of their shoes' since this greatly increases the chance of being in trouble. Also, swinging at maximum speed can upset a golfer's natural rhythm which, once disrupted, can be hard to get back.

A great way of thinking is to fix in your mind that, *a drive is just another layup*. In other words the objective on the tee is to move the ball to a place on the fairway that leaves a straightforward next shot. Smart golfers realise that the game isn't about hitting the ball as far as you can, it's about playing as straight as possible to a favourable location.

The smart golfer also tees his ball at the correct height. Good golfers prize a consistent strike and place the ball on a tee peg at a height that will impact the clubface close to the 'sweet spot' (as opposed to off the bottom or near the top). If you get inconsistent results from good swings on the tee, it might be an idea to rule out variable tee heights as a possible cause.

Many golfers just put their tee pegs in without paying attention. They may even know or 'sense' that the height is wrong, but still do nothing about it. The smart golfer though won't hit a shot if he feels something isn't right – he'll step back, reset the tee height, and approach the ball again.

Working out the optimum height for different clubs is probably best done at the driving range. Once clear on this there are a number of ways to put this into practice. One possibility is to use tee pegs with height markings. Hold the tee in your fingers at the desired height, and push down until you feel the ground, or until the mark meets the earth.

Another possibility is to use 'stepped' tee pegs. These are an even easier way to eliminate variation since they don't require any thought. The step prevents the tee peg from going into the ground beyond the set level. By shopping around you should be able to find a variety of heights to suit your needs.

There is one more point worth mentioning about teeing grounds. Although you might expect all tee boxes to be level, in fact many have significant slope (enough to make a difference). This is difficult to spot because it is unlikely that you will look for it.

One of the courses I regularly play has several tees with a pronounced upslope. From these locations I regularly see a proportion of players failing to get forward to their front foot at the end of a swing. This is most visible when playing a driver, because this shot requires a particularly wide stance. So keep a look out and consider if this might be a problem on any of the holes that you regularly play.

In summary, the smart golfer does everything he can to gain advantage from the opportunity to place the ball on the tee. By prompting himself about this when he steps up onto the tee, he is able to progressively embed good habits into his game.

Occasionally he might check that he is following these principles to good effect, for example by picking a specific round with an objective to check that he does everything right on the tee. Ideally, he would like to be able to give positive answers to the following:

- *Did I seek good grip and balance underfoot and avoid the rough areas on the tee?*
- *Did I optimise the angle of play to best effect?*
- *Did I pick the optimum line and use a divot or other means to aid my alignment?*
- *Did I tee the ball up to the correct height on all my shots?*
- *Did I spot and take account of any slopes on the tee?*
- *Did I make 'normal' swings on uphill and downhill tee shots?*

The answers to these questions should highlight if the player is already 'on top of it', or if further action is required to gain advantage from the tee.

The smart golfer takes the opportunity to position the ball on the tee, finds the best place for the shot, and makes sure he aims well.

SMART GOLFER CHECKLIST – ON THE TEE

- O Avoid bad ground on the tee, use the full depth of the tee
- O Have an aim line for each tee shot
- O Possibly use an old divot hole or ground-mark to line up
- O Select a side of the tee to avoid hazards/feel comfortable
- O Be wary of a dogleg seducing aim
- O Work out the best tee side for all holes on home course
- O Don't swing harder for uphill/downhill tee shots
- O Every drive is *just another layup*
- O Watch out for slopes on tees
- O Always tee up at the correct height

2.   *LIES*

A smart golfer routinely checks his lie and the area underfoot, notes any risks or limitations, and modifies his choice of shot accordingly.

A poor lie restricts the contact that can be made between club and ball. This in turn can restrict what is feasible, or reduce the chances of pulling-off a good shot. Yet when the ball is on the fairway or first cut of rough, many golfers just presume that they have a good lie. They either don't look at the ball, or fail to give it anything more than a cursory glance. But a less than perfect lie is often the sole reason for a bad shot.

Imagine you are playing a long par 4. You've hit a great drive straight down the middle and you are in range of the green. As you approach the ball you are looking forward to the second shot and the possibility of an elusive par on a difficult stroke index. You have already decided to use your 3 wood – all you can think about is hitting the green. When you finally get to the ball you don't look at the lie, or you glance at it, but ignore it. This is easily done – it's on the fairway after all!

Consider another possibility, this time on a short par 4. You have hit a good drive, are on the fairway or in the first cut of semi-rough, and have a full wedge distance to the flag. As you walk up to your ball you only have eyes for the pin. You imagine your shot sailing high in the air and finishing close. The possibility of a birdie beckons. Once again you don't look at the lie – you just assume it's ok.

Yet sometimes the ball will be sitting down in an indentation in the ground, possibly where the grass has grown back over an old divot hole. At other times the path to the back of the ball will be obstructed, perhaps by a small ridge of earth, or a hardened tuft of grass.

In each of these cases there is an increased chance of poor contact, followed by a poor outcome. A normal swing from a 'sitting down lie' will, more often than not, result in either a 'thin' shot (catching the lower part of the clubface only) or a 'fat' shot (hitting the ground first and getting turf between ball and clubface).

With a thin shot the ball will fly low. A thinned fairway wood approach shot would therefore be unlikely to get the full distance, and would perhaps finish in the bunkers short of the green. A thinned wedge shot might run straight through the back of the green. Similarly a fat shot is likely to end up well short. In all cases a dropped-shot beckons.

Checking lies takes a few seconds at most. Yet over a round most golfers would be hard pressed to confirm that they had checked every lie, let alone that they were certain that they'd taken any limitations or risks into account. On your last round how many lies did you look at? Which of these were perfect, average or poor? And did you modify your shot selection based on this?

Consider the situation where a golfer is playing from a bad lie but hasn't noticed it, or has noticed it but not taken it into account. In this instance there is a possibility that the player's sub-conscious is 'aware' of the potential problem, but it hasn't properly registered in the conscious part of his mind.

In this situation a golfer is likely to feel a bit uncomfortable, but not know why. The mind typically handles this type of conflict by raising the golfer's stress level, which in turn creates tension in the body. A smooth swing becomes less likely and the chances of a poor shot increase further.

This feeling that all is not right can occur at any time, not just if you have failed to spot a dodgy lie. If you sense you feel stressed or begin to tense-up when addressing a regular shot, it makes sense to step away and consider what is troubling you. Other examples might be if you don't have the right club, or you can see that even a great strike could end up in trouble because the angles aren't good. Whatever the reason, it makes sense to back off and think again.

The smart golfer therefore always looks at his lies and modifies his shots accordingly. He rigorously adheres to the mantra *don't deny the lie*. He deliberately looks at the lie of the ball and is prepared to act on it. When faced with a less than perfect lie he will make a conscious decision to either go for the shot or not, because he knows that a mistake in this situation will typically cost a shot.

Of course on occasion it is right to be aggressive and take on a risky shot. But for now let's suppose you are playing conservatively; for example, because it is a stroke play round, where every shot counts on the scorecard.

Returning to our example with the long par 4 approach shot where the golfer wants to play a 3 wood, let's assume that the ball is sitting down. The safe option is to take a mid to long iron and layup. Whilst playing the shot it is important to get the clubface as cleanly as possible into the back of the ball, move the ball forward a good distance, and to avoid trouble at all costs.

In the other example, with the wedge approach shot from a bad lie, the golfer might simply aim for a safer part of the green instead of going for the flag. He may even take a line that rules out being on the green, (for example playing to the apron of the green to one side) in return for making his next shot straightforward. The priority is to get as close as possible to the pin, whilst leaving a safe margin for error.

If the plan works, the player will be in a reasonable position with a good frame of mind. Contrast this with a golfer who denied the lie, went for it, tensed up, and ended up in a bunker or in the rough through the back of the green. This player is now struggling and stressed. Who would you expect to score best on this hole?

In some rounds the incidence of bad lies will be higher than for others. In winter when the grass is weak, poor lies will abound (though thankfully preferred lies are played for the worst of this season). In summer when the ground gets baked hard, balls typically only stop rolling and come to rest in slight dips, so playing on courses that don't have much good grass can be quite difficult.

Semi-rough and rough can, of course, always throw up a challenge at any time of year. In contrast a well-manicured course in late spring or early summer is likely to throw up good lies on the fairway nearly all the time (though problems will be more frequent on a poorly maintained course).

If a smart golfer is unable to go for the green, or can't reach it, he will typically 'layup to his favourite distance'. The majority of average golfers tend to not think about this, and many just play a shot with the first club that comes to hand perhaps thinking, *I'll just get it up there as far as I can.* This is a great example of where the smart golfer gains an advantage.

Firstly, he is likely to have a favourite yardage. Several players I play with have settled on 90 yards as being optimum (for them it is a full gap wedge). If the distance is a bit more or less they have the option to take more or less club (using a pitching wedge or a sand wedge), or to grip down or swing a bit more or less. So when they decide to layup, the first thing they think of is playing to a spot about 90 yards from the pin.

Secondly, they make a point of practising shots between 80 and 100 yards on a regular basis. Whilst it seems that they just casually recover from problem situations well, much of what appears to be good skill on the day is as a result of clear thinking and hard work in the past.

At their local range they know which target, or bit of ground, corresponds to their favoured distance and in any session they make sure that they hit at least half a dozen balls to this area. Also if they have time for a few shots before a round, at least one or two will be of this length too.

When considering the lie of the ball, it also makes sense to notice if there are any issues to do with the surface underneath your feet, where you take your stance. A good swing requires a firm foundation. If that is compromised there is a tendency to slip and a poor shot might result.

The smart golfer therefore modifies his shot if, for example, it is from muddy ground, a hard smooth surface, soaking wet grass, leaves or pine needles. The key things to remember are to anchor yourself as best you can and to swing at less than full power (which reduces the chance of slipping). It also makes sense to rehearse the swing on similar terrain nearby; particularly if you don't face this situation often.

It is worth noting that many golfers learn to play and practise their golf at a driving range from perfect lies and ideal underfoot conditions. These players are therefore likely to have a one size fits all swing that is fine for great lies and good ground conditions, but not for problem situations.

From time to time it is an idea to check that you handle 'less than good' lies well. Pick a round and set out to examine all lies and make fully considered shot choices taking these into account. After the round ask yourself:

* *Did I look at and assess every lie, including those that at first glance seemed ok?*

- *Did I take account of any less than perfect lies in my decision-making?*
- *Was my technique playing from less than perfect lies OK, or (preferably) good?*

The best way to improve your play from bad lies is to play shots from them. If you are fortunate your club might have practice facilities where you can do this. Alternatively, at many clubs it is acceptable to play a practice round at a quiet time of the day, so it should be possible to play extra shots from staged locations on the course itself.

Position some balls in old divot holes, dips or places where it is hard to get a good contact with the back of the ball. From these spots play shots with a range of different clubs, for example a 3 wood, hybrid, 6 iron and a wedge. During the process consider just how good (or bad) a lie would have to be for you to go (or not go) for the green in normal circumstances. Also perhaps play some shots from potentially slippery surfaces, for example where there are pine needles or leaves underfoot.

By rehearsing from difficult ground conditions a golfer will be better prepared to meet the challenges faced in a typical round, and almost certainly save a shot or two here and there.

The smart golfer routinely checks his lie and the area underfoot, notes any risks or limitations, and modifies his choice of shot accordingly.

SMART GOLFER CHECKLIST – LIES

- ○ Examine every lie, note if it's poor, average or good
- ○ Accept the constraint – *don't deny the lie*
- ○ When playing from a poor lie factor in the risk
- ○ If uncomfortable at address step away/think again
- ○ From poor lies play away from pins or layup
- ○ Layup to favourite distance(s)
- ○ Examine the surface underfoot
- ○ If slippery, rehearse and play at less than full power
- ○ Practise from bad lies as well as good ones

3.   SLOPES

A smart golfer is fully aware of the slopes around the ball and under his feet, and takes account of this in his shot selection, at address, in his aim, and with his swing.

Golfers who have been brought up on hilly, heavily landscaped, or links courses will be quite used to playing from all manner of slopes. But players who practise their swings solely from flat surfaces (for example from mats at a driving range), typically struggle in comparison. It is no coincidence that many golfers are considerably less accurate with shots from slopes, compared to level ground.

Even golf professionals try to avoid slopes if they can. You will often see them in tournaments taking a lesser club off the tee in order to avoid an approach shot from sloping ground. They know that slopes decrease accuracy in general, and increase the risk of not making good contact with the ball in the first place.

A good proportion of all shots in golf rounds are played from slopes. Holes can be uphill or downhill, and fairways often undulate. There are usually slopes around fairway bunkers, and landscape features that include mounds and dips. Average golfers can therefore easily lose several shots a round playing from slopes. At my home club I regularly see players losing their balance, failing to get a good contact, or simply hitting the ball a long way offline.

The smart golfer knows that slopes are one of golf's big challenges. He makes every effort to ensure that he can play these shots to an adequate standard. Anything he can do to save a shot or two a round has to be worthwhile. So the smart golfer systematically assesses slopes and routinely makes adjustments when playing from them.

There are many different types of slope. Considering one direction at a time there are: 'upslopes' (up towards the target), 'downslopes' (down towards the target), and 'sideslopes' (with the ball either above or below the feet). Then there are slopes that are a combination of either an up or downslope, together with a sideslope.

Each type of slope requires an understanding of the likely difference in ball flight, distance and line (compared to a flat lie). On top of this, adjustments are required to stance, grip and the swing itself. There are therefore many possible situations and many different factors to consider.

The techniques involved in playing from all the different combinations of slope would require lengthy explanation and it is not my intention with this book to discuss the 'swing'. But in case some readers would appreciate an overview of the principles that apply regarding ball flight, stance and grip, I have included a few summary points on these at the end of this chapter.

When faced with a slope, the first task is to assess the extent and direction of it. This might sound obvious, but I repeatedly see average golfers failing to get this right, either by not noticing the slope at all, assuming it is mild when it is severe, or not understanding that there is a second dimension to it. Playing a shot assuming one thing when it is quite another can cause mayhem.

To supplement the assessment with their eyes, some golfers use their sense of balance to 'feel' the ground underneath their feet. They consider which direction they would fall (towards) if they lost their balance. Others imagine the direction a ball would roll if dropped at the spot. In the process, the golfer should also appreciate the extent of the slope – is it mild, average or severe?

Before playing the shot, it makes good sense to rehearse from a similar slope. Retaining good balance throughout is important for any swing, and this is doubly the case when you are not standing on flat ground. When a golfer starts to lose balance, his body automatically reacts to stop him toppling over. This in turn tends to prevent a smooth swing through to the finish.

Since staying in balance is easier with a three-quarter swing, the smart golfer employs this tactic as a matter of course when playing from slopes. In contrast, one of the more dramatic sights on a golf course can be seen when an inexperienced golfer attempts a full power swing from a severe slope without a preceding rehearsal!

So, smart golfers seek to examine each shot to:
- see if it is affected by a slope
- assess the direction and extent of the slope
- make a shot choice taking this into account

He then makes adjustments to aim, stance and swing. Since this is clearly an area where there is much to be gained, it makes sense to maintain these skills and, from time to time, to check that they are being applied well. Whilst playing, the smart golfer should be able to positively answer the following questions:

- *Did I confirm, for every shot, that I was, or was not, on a slope?*
- *Was I clear about the extent and direction of the slope?*
- *For each shot with a significant sloping lie did I allow for the changed ball flight?*
- *Did I make necessary adjustments to my stance, grip and swing?*

These questions make it clear that out on the course the smart golfer knows that it is not just important to examine the lie and slopes, but also to know what to do and (preferably) be confident in his ability to execute.

The acid test with slopes is to check back over your play and see how much less accurate you were with your shots from sloping lies compared to flat ones. If it is material to your game, some work on this is likely to pay dividends.

In the same way as with bad lies, the best way to improve your play from difficult slopes is to play shots from them. Very few clubs have facilities to practise from slopes but if you are lucky enough to have some, do take advantage of this (giving you a real advantage in comparison to golfers who don't have this facility!). Another way to hone your skills is to drop a few extra balls during a practice round at a quiet time of the day.

Perhaps start by playing some shots with the ball above and below your feet. Try a variety of locations and note that in some cases your feet will be on flat ground (making your stance easier) whilst in others your feet will be on sloping ground (making the stance more difficult). Also play some shots from up and down slopes.

You may also find it useful to occasionally check that you are reading slopes correctly. During a round, pause either before or after some of your shots and pay extra attention to the ground. If you think there is no slope, double check that this is in fact the case. If there is a slope, double check it's extent and line. I do this from time to time and am continually surprised that I fail to spot some slopes at all, and I consistently underestimate others.

If you either can't get on the course to practise, or don't have the time, some shots can be simulated from mats or flat ground at the range by playing balls from 'altered positions'. For example you might:
- lean away from the target, onto the back foot (to simulate an upslope)
- lean towards the target, onto the front foot (to mimic a downslope)
- stand more or less upright and grip up or down (for ball above or below feet)
- use a closed/open clubface (simulating the flight of a ball above/below the feet)

As this discussion shows, playing from slopes is a complex subject. It therefore makes sense to seek help if it is a problem in your game. The good news is that the principles that apply are founded on common sense. Once appreciated, they should be easy to remember and repeat on the course.

One possible solution is to seek out video clips demonstrating the four main possibilities (upslope, downslope, and the two sideslopes). Otherwise, find a golfer who plays well from slopes and ask them to show you what they do. Or speak with a golf professional who should easily be able to put you on the right track.

To summarise, the situations we face out on the golf course contain far more variety than we encounter at the range, particularly in respect of slopes. Being mindful of this whilst practising and when making choices and executing shots, helps to make a better golfer. So the ground matters.

The smart golfer is fully aware of the slopes around the ball and under his feet, and takes account of this in his shot selection, at address, in his aim, and with his swing.

SMART GOLFER CHECKLIST – SLOPES

- ◯ Check for slopes on every shot, extent and line
- ◯ Rehearse before playing from slopes
- ◯ Adjust stance, setup and aim
- ◯ Use a three-quarter swing
- ◯ Practise from slopes

PRINCIPLES OF PLAYING FROM SLOPES – BALL FLIGHT

On a downslope the ball flies lower (so less club is required for the same distance). On an upslope the ball flies higher (shots therefore need more club).

With a ball above the feet, it will tend to fly left and further than normal (some players compensate for this by opening the clubface a bit at address, others simply aim somewhat to the right).

With a ball below the feet, it will tend to fly to the right and travel less distance than normal (some players compensate for this by closing the clubface a bit at address, others simply aim more to the left).

PRINCIPLES OF PLAYING FROM SLOPES – STANCE AND GRIP

The general principle with stance is to adjust to 'match the slope'. This is important since it improves the chances of making a clean contact with the ball. On a downslope (or upslope), this is achieved by tilting the spine towards (or away from) the target.

For a sideslope with the ball above the feet, a golfer will typically stand more upright and slide his hands down the grip (this compensates for the fact that the ball is closer to the shoulders in comparison to playing from flat ground).

For a sideslope with the ball below the feet, a golfer will typically bend over more, and possibly slide his hands up towards the end of the grip (to compensate for the increased distance to the ball).

ACCURACY

Golf is a game of accuracy. Players select a target (allowing for a margin of error), calculate the distance (allowing for wind and elevation) and match this with a yardage, club and shot combination (using a full or partial swing).

4.   DISTANCES

A smart golfer works out distances efficiently, makes sound club selections, and gets good feedback on the distance of his shots.

After selecting a target, the smart golfer swiftly and accurately works out the distance to it. This gives him more time to decide what shot to play and which club to take. Over the ball he is confident that he has the right yardage. After the shot he can assess if he struck the ball well by seeing if it went the correct distance.

On the other hand, a golfer who struggles to estimate distances can feel rushed and stressed, particularly if the calculation isn't straightforward. He might also fail to come up with the correct number. If he is uncertain about the yardage, he is less likely to get a good result. As he settles over the ball he may still have doubts about whether he has the right club in hand.

Golfers who make the wrong calculation, or who settle for a rough approximation, are also left with a problem after the event. Let's say the ball comes up short or long. That might be as a result of a good shot with a bad yardage, or as a result of a bad shot with a good yardage! In comparison, golfers who have reliable feedback on shot outcomes gain valuable information to help them learn and improve.

The most frequent measurement needed is to the centre of the green from the fairway or light rough, or from the tee on a par 3. Par 3s have plates, discs or signs on the tees that show distances to the centre of the greens. On par 4s and 5s, many clubs have marker posts to one side of the fairway, such as at 150 yards, or coloured discs in the centre of fairways, for example at 100, 150 and 200 yards.

Note that in some cases these measurements are to the front of the greens, instead of the middle. So if you are playing an unfamiliar course, do check which system they use. Some courses also have precise yardages marked on sprinkler heads and these again tend to be to the front of the green.

It is a great help if your ball comes to rest next to one of these markers. But what if there is no information at all? Clearly a GPS unit (Global Positioning System) or laser range finder would help, but for now let's assume that you don't have one with you. The possibilities that remain are pacing out the distance, or estimating with your eyes.

Estimating the distance to the pin from the fairway is often done by pacing out the distance, for example from the 150-yard marker, and adding or subtracting from this. But estimating by pacing can easily produce the wrong result. The most common error is with the length of stride.

It is perhaps not surprising that the length of our paces varies with the speed we walk, though few golfers take this into account in practice. When you walk quickly your pace length is completely different to when you are ambling along. I first noticed when I played two consecutive rounds: one when I was taking my time on a fine summer evening; and the other when I was rushing and under time pressure.

At normal walking pace an average stride for me is just over a yard. But seven of my fast paces equals ten of my slow ones. In other words, I could be 10 yards out with a typical measurement (say over 30 paces). This in turn could for me be the difference between getting a par or a bogey.

If you regularly pace out distances, it is helpful to fix in your mind a 'normal pace', and to re-confirm it from time to time. A way to do this is to count your strides between two of the markers, or from one of the markers to the green. Was this the number of steps you expected? Try walking faster or slower. What is the variation?

Estimating with your eyes can also be problematic. For me what looks like 20 yards one day, can look like 25 or 30 the next (perhaps that's just some problem I have, but I suspect not!). Also, downhill can appear to be further than it really is, and uphill shorter. This is particularly the case if it is a gradually increasing or decreasing slope, in other words where the incline or decline isn't constant.

There might also be an angle to be considered from your reference point. For example the 150-yard post could be on the other side of the fairway. Or your ball might be on one edge of the fairway whereas the disc is in the centre. To make things worse, the markers on courses are occasionally not accurate. The combined effect can easily result in a golfer being 10 or 20 yards out with their calculation, causing a possible shot loss.

One member of my home club is a master of distance despite being a complete technophobe – he'd sooner give up golf than get a GPS or laser-finder. Instead, as a one-off exercise, he worked out a number of set-distances on the course, measuring from landmarks such as posts, trees, bushes and bunker edges.

For example on some holes he knows the distance from the back tee to:
- avoid being blocked by the big oak tree
- carry the fairway bunker
- stay short of the run-out area
- stay short of the fairway bunkers
- reach the centre of the dogleg

On other holes, he knows the distance from a fairway marker, or landscape feature such as a distinctive bush or the edge of a fairway bunker to:
- carry the water, straight and 'on the angle'
- the start and end of the layup area on a par 5, avoiding difficulty short and long
- clear the lip of the bunkers guarding the front of greens
- layup short of the water

He adjusts the numbers in his head by the number of paces he has walked past the landmark and this helps him easily decide which shot to play.

Whilst a painstaking approach like this might seem a bit daunting to some, you might nevertheless consider if it would be useful if you knew a few set-distances like these on your home course. For example, are there locations where you find you repeatedly have to make calculations, and don't always get them right?

If you can relate to this, then a one-time measuring exercise may save you shots or repeated effort in the future. Take the time in a round to measure some distances and make a note of them. With frequent use they will soon fix in your mind.

For approach shots, the location of the pin on the green is an extra factor in the calculation. This can be more or less of an issue depending on the size of the greens. Several of the courses I play have smallish greens, a maximum of 20 paces across. But one club I play several times a year has no fewer than ten greens measuring between 35 and 45 yards from front to back!

Many golf courses use a system to help with pin locations: flags are given different colours to designate front, middle and back, or a smaller second flag is put on the flagstick showing much the same thing. Some clubs also provide information on pin-sheets. For shots into long greens this information can be most valuable.

With all these possibilities for inaccuracy it is easy to understand why GPS units and laser range-finders are so popular. Instead of having to do calculations (which may in themselves be incorrect), it is generally just a question of reading one figure, which should be fairly accurate.

Some GPS units also display a map of the hole and allow the golfer to move a cursor on the screen to the point he wishes to play to. The unit then automatically shows the distance to the marked point and the distance from the marked point to the centre of the green.

With these devices you can even move the cursor to the pin position (such as back left or front right) for more accuracy.

If the shot is a drive, the GPS allows you to see how far you can go before getting into trouble, and the distance you need to carry to avoid a bunker. This type of unit also calculates the remaining distance to the green after your initial shot – a feature that is most helpful for laying-up to a favourite yardage.

In some ways GPS units have the edge over range-finders. A range-finder's 'sight system' can be prone to error when reading to anything other than a flag or a solid object (such as a tree trunk). Looking at an area of grass, with no sharply defined edge or distinguishing feature, might result in an incorrect reading. A further negative is that the range-finder is not able to give readings to targets that are out of sight, for example if the flag is over the brow of a hill or behind some trees.

On the other hand, a range-finder gives a simple one-off read to an un-obstructed flag, and no compensation is required for pin position (unlike with a GPS). This makes range-finders popular with golfers who tend to aim at or near the pin, as opposed to the centre of the green.

The range-finder is also helpful for practising distance control, for example at the driving range where you can readily see how far targets are from your playing area.

I know that many golfers will resist the suggestion of getting a device, possibly because they have managed perfectly well up until now without one. But if you want to get really good, or even just not miss any opportunity to score better, it makes sense to get a helping hand. I know many golfers who held back from getting a GPS unit, only to say when they have one that it is one of the best things they have ever bought.

Using a GPS or range finder not only increases accuracy, but also cuts down on time, and just as importantly, mental effort. I find that it really comes into its own when I am well out of position and thus need to know an unusual distance to the green or to a specific point on the fairway (for example to layup to my favourite wedge distance). It can also be really helpful for shot selection decisions on unfamiliar courses.

The downside to using technology is perhaps that carrying something extra around or getting any device out of your pocket or bag can be a bit of a hassle. But most players now attach their units to their bags or trolleys, and soon learn to get readouts quickly (and increasingly golf carts are being equipped with these).

If you still don't like the sound of a large unit, a GPS watch is another option. These generally work well, are unobtrusive, and always with you (though in winter it can be a bit of a problem checking it under heavy or tight fitting clothing).

Whatever you do, it is hopefully clear that correctly knowing distances is a core element in being able to plot your way around a golf course to best effect.

The smart golfer works out distances efficiently, makes sound club selections, and gets good feedback on the distance of his shots.

SMART GOLFER CHECKLIST – DISTANCES

O   Always be clear about the distance to the target
O   When using steps, walk at a known pace
O   If estimating by eye, check this sometimes
O   Be wary of measuring 'on the angle' from posts/markers
O   Watch out for long greens – pin positions are key
O   Consider using a GPS or range finder
O   Or work out some home course set-distances

5.   CLUB-YARDAGES

A smart golfer knows his club-yardages and the likely spread of his shots, and uses this information to navigate around the course.

Knowing how far you hit the ball with your standard swing, with different clubs, is absolutely fundamental to playing good golf. The same goes for understanding how straight or wayward you tend to be. A golfer with a good appreciation of his likely accuracy is better able to safely plot his way around the golf course.

A key point here is that the main determinant of your score tends to be *the effect of your poor shots, not the good ones*. On average, a player who doesn't hit any great shots from tee to green, but who is rarely far off track, will outscore a player of the same general ability, who hits some great shots, but is way offline (or long or short) with others.

The smart golfer sets out to plot his way around the course minimising the chance of getting into trouble and thus losing strokes. He aims his shots into target areas (such as fairway spaces and greens), allowing enough leeway for his personal margin for error.

In order to do this well, he needs to know the distance to his targets (as per the last chapter), the distance he hits each of his clubs, and roughly how accurate he is with these on average (in terms of being long, short, left or right).

Knowing the average yardages for each club also speeds-up club and shot selection on the course. If you have need to debate or guess what club will get you to a target, this will cost thinking time and might allow indecision to creep in. But many golfers only have a rough idea of their own club-yardages.

With full swings in the summer my 'carries' with each club are approximately:

Driver	= 230
3 wood	= 215
Hybrid	= 195
4 iron	= 180
5 iron	= 170
6 iron	= 160
7 iron	= 150
8 iron	= 140
9 iron	= 130
Pitching wedge	= 115
Gap wedge	= 100
Sand wedge	= 85
Lob wedge	= 65

I know that my iron and hybrid yardages are fairly correct because I check them every now and then. It is a straightforward job to play to a level par 3 on a day with no wind and to log the distance the ball flew in the air. Another possibility is to hit some extra balls on the course using the 100, 150 and 200-yard markers as a guide, or to use a GPS if you have one.

It would also be nice to think that a driving range could help in this respect; after all they generally have targets with yardages marked on. But there are several reasons to be cautious with this.

Some ranges are up or downhill, which means an adjustment in the first place. Also, the numbers on range-targets are often not correct (many ranges move these around and the distances will change over time) and the actual distances to targets will vary depending on which bay you are in. Finally, many range balls are distance limited, so normal balls are likely to travel further in regular play.

If you know your yardages well this will help greatly with approach shots, including at unfamiliar courses where you might not have built up the knowledge of what club to take on a par 3. It is a good idea to create a list showing your 'carry' for each club with full shots, similar to the one above. Doing so will help fix them in your mind and this will, in turn, cut down your thinking time on the course.

It is not unusual for even experienced golfers to repeatedly come up short time and time again. This seems to be because the numbers they have fixed in their minds are the yardages achieved for their 'very best' shots. If you want to score well it is important to be realistic. Use the average, not the maximum.

As you list your yardages there are a couple more points to consider about balls. Firstly your choice of ball can affect distances greatly. So when you measure make sure it is with the ball you usually play with. Secondly, there is generally a loss of distance in winter when the air is cold, and at any time when the air is damp. So adjustments are required in these conditions.

Most golfers' yardages don't change much once they have an established swing. But a successful swing change might result in an increase in distance, as might a change of clubs or ball. And senior golfers will inevitably have to accept a decline in the length of their shots over time.

The other element that makes up accuracy is the distribution of shots from left to right. Imagine playing ten shots from the same spot to the same target. Some will be short, others long, or to the left or right of the target. Your 'spread' is the area that your shots cover.

Ideally a golfer's left/right distribution should be even, with as many balls to the left as right, at similar distances from the target-line on both sides. In the same way, the short/long distribution should ideally also be even, with as many balls short as long, and with an equal spread of distances on both sides.

You can check your spread by hitting ten shots with the same club at the range. But beware that in doing so you will tend to build up a rhythm that could make it unrepresentative of what happens during a round. Additionally, you might unknowingly begin to compensate, for example if the majority of your balls start coming up short, or to one side of the target.

Most golfers hitting ten shots in a row, with the same aim and posture, will have more on one side than the other. Similarly, most golfers will have more balls short than long. In the rare instance where you are even on both sides, and have as many shots long as short, give yourself a gold star!

It can be beneficial to understand what spread you achieve on the course. Take, for example, your last ten approach shots with irons. Were there as many long as short, and to the right as left? I suspect many golfers would benefit by working this out. I repeatedly see golfers with a fade coming up about a club short, and off to the right. If they merely took a club more, and aimed at the left edge of the green, most of their shots would end up a lot closer to the centre of the green.

So it makes sense to have good knowledge about your club-yardages and accuracy. Understanding your own spread, and adjusting your aim and club selection away from trouble based on this, can produce immediate benefits.

The smart golfer knows his club-yardages and the likely spread of his shots, and uses this information to navigate around the course.

SMART GOLFER CHECKLIST – CLUB-YARDAGES

O   Work out and write down full swing yardages
O   Be realistic, use average numbers not maximums
O   Understand typical spread and adjust if needs be
O   Match target areas to club-yardages and spread

6. SHOT VARIATION

A smart golfer has a consistent three-quarter swing, and is able to adjust the length of his shots, particularly within 'scoring' range.

Walking up to the ball, it is always satisfying to see that the yardage to the pin is the exact number for a favourite club. But what if it's in-between? Many golfers will stick with a full swing and take one more (or less) club. This is fine if you are happy with the full increased (or decreased) distance. But what if this brings trouble into play?

Many golfers give the swing a bit more to get more distance. But typically this approach often produces a less accurate shot, either in length, direction, or both. Forcing a shot like this can also upset your rhythm.

For less distance a golfer could simply swing a bit less hard. But this too can produce problems, for example by 'quitting on the shot'.

Another way to get less distance is to take a full swing but 'choke-down' – sliding the hand down the grip an inch or so. For an average golfer this should result in a loss of about 5 – 10 yards when compared to a full swing. The same gripping-down approach can also be used for *extra* distance – take 'one more club' and grip down a bit. In my experience 'gripping down' tends on average to produce a more consistent outcome than just taking a bit off the shot.

Shots from 40 – 100 yards are particularly important to scoring well – hence this area is often called the 'scoring zone'. The smart golfer knows this and has learned to vary his shot lengths within this range. A good result from this distance usually means that the player hits the green (or fringe at a minimum) and gets down in three shots, occasionally two. But a player missing the green is likely to take four shots. If this happens just once or twice in a round the cost can soon add up.

Average sets of clubs these days have three wedges. The gaps between these clubs with full swings might be 20 yards or more, ironically in the area that is arguably most critical to scoring well. So golfers need the ability to adjust the length of their shots. The gripping-down approach helps, but something more is needed.

Some talented players are blessed with great skill and judgement, and can just swing harder or softer to hit any number. But most golfers find a 'system' works better. If you struggle with accuracy in this range it makes sense to develop a consistent partial swing.

A useful tool to have in your armoury is a repeatable three-quarter swing, so named because the club is swung three-quarters of the way back, or with three-quarters power. This immediately gives several more yardage options.

I learned this shot at a driving range with full-length bay mirrors. I began by hitting balls with a pitching wedge at (what seemed to me to be) half or three-quarters of my normal power. In the mirror I noted that my left arm came up to about 9 o'clock on the scale of a clock face at the top of the swing (where 6 o'clock is vertical, with the arms and hands pointing down at address).

Next I continued to hit balls, concentrating on getting a good rhythm, a clean strike and a consistent distance. When I settled on a partial swing that felt comfortable and repeatable, I once again noted my left arm position in the mirror. This time it was consistently just past horizontal at the top of my swing.

Using this swing with my pitching wedge, I hit the ball almost exactly 75% of my normal full-swing distance. Whether it's exactly three-quarters or a bit less or a bit more, is not important. The critical thing is that you can repeat this swing length and shot distance with ease.

Once ingrained, a swing like this can be used to produce even more distances by:
- gripping up or down a bit at address
- swinging a bit higher up or lower down the clock face
- playing these shots with other clubs (such as your gap wedge and 9 iron)

With practice, using two or three clubs, and with simple modifications, most golfers should be able to ultimately create a 'system' where they can 'call-up' shots that travel roughly 40, 50, 60, 70, 80 and 90 yards in the air.

If you currently struggle from 100 yards and in and can get this system to work, your scores might improve dramatically. Refining this over time, you should hardly ever miss a green, not to mention being able to more often get the ball in 'birdie territory'.

Whilst learning to play shots with partial swings, it obviously helps to have a set of targets of varying distances, where you know the distances are correct. Some ranges and practice areas have flags and targets at specific distances, but others will have targets with no distance information at all.

For this reason, if distance control is really important to you, I suggest getting hold of a range-finder. This way you can setup to a target at any range or practice area, from any angle, and be sure that you have the exact distance, thus getting the best possible feedback on your accuracy.

In addition to the benefit of having more club/yardage options, the three-quarter swing is a great tool to have in windy conditions. Into a strong breeze a slightly mis-hit full shot may go well off line and lose much of its distance.

A three-quarter shot though, will be affected much less. The reason for this is the higher spin produced by a full shot – the greater the spin the more the wind affects the golf ball in flight. In fact in windy conditions good golfers tend to play more partial than full shots overall.

The same technique can be used for longer distances using other clubs such as a 6 or 5 iron. Though, as you might discover, many players find that it is a much greater challenge to master this with longer clubs.

Players who are able to 'call up' shots that fly a required distance for shots of less than 100 yards are able to score better. Therefore the smart golfer makes the effort to develop a consistent three-quarter swing. To maintain this, he periodically visits a driving range, and plays a variety of shots, with different clubs, to known distances.

The smart golfer has a consistent three-quarter swing, and is able to adjust the length of his shots, particularly within 'scoring' range.

SMART GOLFER CHECKLIST – SHOT VARIATION

○ Have a repeatable partial swing, e.g. three-quarter length
○ Maintain this with practice, as required
○ Be able to vary the swing up and down the clock face
○ Use grip-down variations to adjust for more distances
○ Practise to known distances, perhaps using a range-finder
○ Use partial swings into wind for less spin and deviation
○ Extend this to long irons to increase shot options

7.   *WIND AND ELEVATION*

A smart golfer understands wind and elevation effects, and handles these well.

For different golfers, wind may be more or less of a challenge. If you regularly play on links or other exposed courses you are likely to be on top of this already. Similarly if you have a low ball flight, or aren't particularly long, it will be less of a problem. In my case I tend to hit the ball long and high, often with a fade, sometimes in very strong winds. So it's a big deal for me.

With wind there are two factors to consider – strength and direction. It's a good idea to get a feel for these even before you arrive at the course. A weather website will show you what's expected for each locality, giving wind strength and direction at (say) three-hourly intervals. This information is not always accurate, but it does provide a good starting point.

The smart golfer also makes a point of knowing the rough compass-orientation of holes on a course. He therefore has a good idea of the likely impact of a given-wind on his club and shot selections in advance. If the wind is strong he might even have made provisional club selection decisions for some holes. The smart golfer knows that the more he can think things through before he plays, the better.

Those players who find wind troublesome, or who play the game to a high standard, need a means of estimating strength and direction on the spot. The wind can get up one minute and die-down the next, or change direction at a moment's notice. The usual way of doing this is to release a pinch of grass at shoulder height and watch the direction and angle it falls to the ground. Racing clouds will also give an indication, as will the angle that the flag is flying on the pin.

Wind strength is usually described in golfers' language as being 1, 2 or 3 'extra clubs'. In this definition a '1 club wind against' means that you need one more club when playing straight into it, in other words you might need a 7 iron instead of an 8. Incidentally, for most people a 10 mph equates to about one more club, and 20 mph is two more, etc.

If you want to get a good handle on this you might consider checking things out during a quiet round on a day when there's a steady strong wind of perhaps 10 or 20 mph. Firstly look up the average wind strength and direction, then out on the course, check the angle of grass-fall in several locations. Does this correlate with what you'd expect?

If wind significantly impacts your game, it also makes sense to properly understand the effect that it has on your shots. Take a club that you know goes a certain distance, for example a 9 iron carrying 110 yards. To understand the effect, hit several balls directly into, for example, a 20mph wind and take the average, or just note the distance travelled by a single shot that you felt was normal. Then do the same downwind.

In a 20 mph wind an average golfer will typically find that his shots go about 15 – 20 yards less upwind, and about 10 yards further downwind. The reason for the difference is that wind interacts more with a golf ball's spin upwind, than it does downwind.

Then perhaps try this in a 20 mph crosswind. A straight hitter's ball will probably deviate sideways by about 10 yards. Golfers with a fade will find that the effect is very different depending on the side the wind comes from. If the wind is left to right (in the direction of the fade for a right-handed golfer), a full shot may end up 20 or even 25 yards off line, and be short by 10 or so yards.

In contrast, a right to left wind will work to cancel out the fade effect. The deviation off line might therefore be minimal, but there will still be some distance loss.

There is another effect of wind that is less well appreciated. In windy conditions many players find that they become tense. This can create a swing problem, which in turn will produce poor shots, and possibly create a downwards spiral into poor play generally. There are several reasons for this.

Firstly, it's a normal instinct to sense the need to hit the ball harder into wind than if it was calm. This can result in the spectre of golfers on the tee, with their drivers, trying to 'come out of their shoes' or 'knock the cover off the ball'. The resulting strike is rarely 'pure' and usually produces a higher amount of ball spin. A wind, particularly a headwind, multiplies the effect of any shortcoming.

Secondly, the mere presence of wind and gusts can cause players to tense up, possibly because of the wind's noise, or the background of constantly moving leaves, branches and long grass. Once again the swing might suffer. The antidote to these problems seems straightforward, but is actually not easy to master.

The golfer needs to somehow retain a normal rhythm and not hit any shots harder than he would in normal conditions. Thus many players adopt the mantra, *if it's breezy, swing easy*. This can be difficult to achieve in practice, but if you can master the approach, it will stand you in good stead.

Since it can be difficult to keep your balance with the wind blowing you all over the place, some golfers also widen their stance a bit to create a more solid foundation.

In addition to wind, elevation change needs to also be taken into account when calculating the 'effective distance' to the target. If there is an elevation change between where you are standing, and where you want the ball to finish, some adjustment will be required.

The majority of courses I play have several holes where you play upwards or downwards to the green. One of these has no fewer than six holes where the approach shot is severely uphill or downhill. If I judge these shots well I know I will score better than if I don't.

If an uphill green has a gently sloping entrance and a relatively flat and trouble-free surround, the calculation is straightforward. A 'slight' slope might be half a club difference, 'medium' could be one full club, and a 'severe' slope might be as much as one and a half or even two clubs more.

It can help to give elevated shots and holes you play regularly a 'rating' based on the number of clubs more or less it requires to reach them on a day with no wind. Once you have these numbers fixed in your mind, club selection decisions will be easier. I regularly see average golfers on the tee at my home course pondering how much less or more club to take, even in perfectly still conditions (despite the fact that they have played this hole most weeks for many years).

Some uphill greens have a severely sloping front and a 'lip'. If the ball doesn't clear this, it will run back down the hill and the resulting chip could be problematic (for example, standing on a steep slope unable to see the landing area, or even the pin at all). So for shots to uphill greens with sloping fronts the priority is to make sure you clear the lip. Failing to do so can cost a shot.

A downhill green in normal conditions is perhaps a more straightforward challenge. If there is a slope down into the green and a normal amount of 'run', it should be possible to fly the ball either direct onto the surface or drop it just short (so it rolls forwards gently onto the green). The margin for error to finish on the putting surface can therefore be larger than usual.

Sometimes the separate challenges of wind and elevation combine to make things even more difficult. My home course has two par 3s with elevated tees that present a massive challenge from time to time. The first has a 190-yard carry over water. The second is a mere 130 yards, but with quite a drop from tee to green. Both face southwest into the prevailing wind and if there is a strong headwind it plays havoc with scoring.

On these two holes, two things become apparent about the strength and effect of the wind. Firstly, because you are 'higher-up', the wind is often stronger on the tee than it is at green level (as verified by the grass-test). Secondly, because the ball spends longer in the air (since it has more distance to fall from the top of its flight), it is affected more. The combination of these factors in a very strong wind can be devastating.

There is one last point to make about the impact of the air on the ball. A shot will often fly less far over a stretch of water. There are several technical reasons for this, but suffice to say that if you are playing over water and sense that the air is swirling around, it is a good idea to take an extra club.

There are no easy solutions for handling the wind. But the general principle of flighting the ball lower, with less spin, tends to produce the best results. Getting this right involves some trial and error but, once mastered, should pay dividends.

In order to crack problems like this, there is no substitute for playing a handful of balls from troublesome spots on a windy day, trying out different combinations of shots and clubs. Getting a feel for how to play shots from key positions on your home course can be very helpful, particularly at a time when you most need to deliver on a critical shot in an important round.

The smart golfer understands wind and elevation effects, and handles these well.

SMART GOLFER CHECKLIST – WIND AND ELEVATION

O   Look up wind strength and direction before arriving to play
O   Know where North, South, East, West are on home course
O   In strong wind, consider provisional club selections pre-round
O   Understand the 1,2,3-club wind approach including grass drop
O   Maintain inner calm and keep tension out of the body
O   Swing easy with a normal rhythm
O   Modify 'effective target distance' for wind and elevation
O   Always aim to clear lips to uphill greens
O   Understand that elevation multiplies the wind's effect
O   Note that wind strength can vary over water; be cautious
O   Practise club/shot/swing combinations at key spots

CONSISTENCY

Consistency is the hallmark of a good player. Many golfers' attempts to achieve this are undermined by poor aim and alignment, and by variations in setup and posture.

8.   AIM AND ALIGNMENT

A smart golfer has a precise target and aim-line, and lines up well.

Good aim and alignment are critical to good golf. Yet many golfers just walk up to the ball, glance in the direction they want the ball to go, and fire away. As a result there is a good chance they will line up incorrectly and a good swing could produce a great shot down the wrong line!

In order to aim correctly there are two things to consider: the target-line and the aim-line. Let's say we have a clear target, for example the pin at the centre of a large level green on a calm day. In this instance the target-line and aim-line are both 'the flag'.

If there is a crosswind, the target is still the flag, but the aim-line will be somewhere to the left or right of it. Similarly if the green has a steady slope from one side to the other, the aim-line will again be to one side of the target (to allow the ball to roll down to the pin).

The aim-line will also be different to the target-line for golfers with an 'institutional shot shape'. On a calm day a player with a fade will start his shot off to the left of the target, and the curved shape will hopefully bring the ball back the required amount. Irrespective of whether you hit the ball straight or with 'shape', it makes sense to think in terms of both a target and an aim-line.

Studies have shown that it is important to be as precise as possible with your aim-line. The key thing is to have a clear picture in your mind of the initial track of ball, so you can setup square to this.

With approach shots it is usually easy to pick out an aim-line. There are normally features around a green such as slopes, edges, hazards and the flag that provide good definition to help with this. For approach shots the line could, for example, be the 'left edge of the green', 'the trunk of the large tree at the back' or the flag itself.

However, finding an object to aim at for a drive, or for a layup to a par 5, is sometimes not so easy. In most instances there will still be a feature that will do the trick (such as a stake in the middle of the fairway, a bunker, or a tree in the background). But other times a golfer will be stuck with just the fairway.

If this is the case the average golfer more often than not sets up roughly for (what he thinks is) the middle of the fairway or layup area, then pulls the trigger. There are two problems with this.

Firstly, it is not easy to line up well with something that is vaguely defined. The line that the golfer 'assumes' is the centre may easily be to one side or the other. Secondly, lining up to a vague target can result in a sloppy attempt to do so, particularly if the player knows that *there's plenty of space down there* after all.

The smart golfer, on the other hand, is more precise. He has learnt that lining up vaguely to a vague target is asking for trouble. He also knows that fixing a specific aim-line or target in his mind's eye increases the chances of getting close to it. It's no surprise to him to see average golfers aiming or lining up poorly, then going way off line (with what seemed to be a perfectly good shot with a perfectly good swing).

So the smart golfer makes sure he always has a precise point to aim at. Some golfers pick out an intermediate spot on the ground within a few feet of the ball (as per the approach suggested earlier in Chapter 1 – On the Tee). This spot might be an old divot, tuft of grass, or some grass with a slightly different shade.

Standing behind the ball, looking down the aim-line, he'll look at the spot, move in, and align his clubface and body square to it at address. Incidentally, this method is used by many for all their shots as part of their overall 'routine', even when there is also a clear target to aim for.

Others look for something to align with in the distance. This could be at ground level (for example a bunker or bush in the distance), or on the horizon (for example the top of the leftmost tree on the horizon). If the background is featureless, the golfer might revert to the 'intermediate spot' approach.

I mentioned setting up 'square to the line' and this requires a bit of clarification. Some golfers setup square to where they want the ball to end up, but then shuffle their stance a bit left or right to allow for their fade or the crosswind. Whatever you do, the key thing is to have a clear approach to the task, and to do this consistently.

A golfer who knows he has lined up properly, knows he has the best chance of success. To look at it the other way around, if he hasn't lined up rigorously then from time to time he will be lined up wrong. And he will never know if the cause of an offline shot was his swing, alignment, or something else all together. Hence, when an apparently good shot goes offline, the first question a smart golfer asks is, *was I aimed and lined up well?*

Whilst discussing aim and alignment, I should mention a particular problem that can cause even disciplined golfers to misalign on the tee from time to time. Many golfers just set up square to the tee boxes. After all these should point down the fairway to the best landing area, or to the centre of the green on a par 3. But this is not always the case. I quite often see good golfers play a great shot down the wrong line having been seduced by this (myself included!).

A slightly different problem can crop-up on modern courses that have one long teeing ground for some holes. These oblong 'islands' are designed to create different angles and a variety of distances to the landing area or green. Their edges may therefore point well to the left or right of the centre line. This can seduce the player into lining up wrong, much the same as with non-square tee boxes. The smart golfer is watchful for both of these situations.

During a round it is hard to check if you've lined up well since ideally you need to see yourself in position from behind. The best that can be done is to setup to your aim-line, place a club shaft along your shoulder, hips or foot line, and judge if this is pointing at the line you wish the ball to start on (you may see other golfers doing this from time to time too). Alternatively you could ask a fellow player to check how you are doing.

But it should be noted that many golfers' natural setups point somewhat to the left or right, instead of square. Some players setup with the fronts of their feet not square to each other – for example the left foot might be out in front of the right (perhaps to promote a draw), or the left foot might be splayed towards the target (perhaps to promote a better follow-through). Similarly some players' hips and shoulders might naturally be somewhat 'open', or 'closed'.

To consistently aim and align well, it is best to have a routine as you address the ball. There are many approaches but the key elements are to ensure you have:
- a clear target
- a precise aim-line
- a point to setup to (either a near spot or one in the distance)
- good alignment to this point

Many players find they achieve this best by always standing a few yards behind the ball before they move in to address. This allows them to confirm the target and the aim-line, and to pick out a spot and move in purposefully to align with it.

Some players also find it helpful to hold their club out in front of them before they move in, squinting with one eye, letting the shaft form a line covering the ball and the aim-point. This reinforces the line of play in the mind's eye, and helps with visualising the shot. You will see a good number of playing professionals doing this in tournaments on TV.

To help ingrain the method of spot alignment (where you align with a spot a few feet in front as opposed to something on the horizon), one player I know uses pebbles at the driving range. Before he settles down to practise he places half a dozen stones at different angles in front of the playing area or mat. These are arranged to provide good coverage of the lines of play to the targets on the range.

Before each shot he stands behind the ball and holds his club up, pointing between the ball and his aim-line. The shaft either covers a pebble, or forms a line which runs an inch or two either side of one. He then walks in from behind, and aligns his clubface and body with the spot. This approach enables him to re-enforce his setup routine, and make his practice session more meaningful.

One point to note with the spot-aiming method is that the spot should not be too far in front of the ball. Ideally it should be in your field of vision so that you can still see it without having to turn your head or body at address. If you do turn your body or head (perhaps to double check before you start your swing), there is a danger that you will not turn fully back afterwards, and you might then swing with an unintentionally open stance.

It should be clear that a consistent approach to aim and alignment is important. Whilst practising, it makes sense to play shots to specific targets and to make a definite attempt to line up well. If you can develop a routine that works well, it will produce benefits over and over again, and potentially last you a lifetime.

Aiming poorly or lining up wrong is perhaps the biggest cause of offline shots from a good swing. So this has to be worth getting right and checking from time to time.

The smart golfer has a precise target, a clear aim-line, and lines up well.

SMART GOLFER CHECKLIST – AIM AND ALIGNMENT

- O   Ensure good aim and alignment for all shots
- O   Target-line and aim-line are two different things
- O   Setup to the aim-line, not the target-line
- O   Have a precise aim-line, e.g. a feature of the terrain
- O   Ideally walk in from behind
- O   Consider using the aim-spot technique
- O   Check body alignment sometimes, perhaps with help
- O   Practise aim and alignment

9.   *SETUP AND POSTURE*

A smart golfer knows that variations in setup and posture produce variations in the swing, and inevitably result in inconsistent golf.

Good setup is one of the fundamentals of good golf. By setup I mean a golfer's positioning immediately prior to starting the swing. The expression, *what you set is what you get,* is more valid than many golfers realise.

A poor setup can produce any manner of problems. In fact, it almost guarantees that your swing won't be good. Yet many golfers happily work on their swings without considering whether their setup or posture might be one reason, or even *the sole reason,* for their current problems.

The 'setup' comprises many different elements including:
- the grip (hand position and grip pressure)
- feet position (stance width and feet angle to the aim-line)
- being anchored (a solid base with active legs)
- ball position in relation to the body (the distance to the ball)
- ball position in relation to the feet (the extent forward or backward in the stance)
- the extent of bend (the angle of tilt forward from the hips)
- the extent of spine tilt away from the target
- arm, shoulder and head positions
- angle of the body to the aim-line (square, a bit open or closed)

From this list it is easy to see that an inconsistent setup can produce all manner of problems. So if a smart golfer wants to improve his swing, or solve a problem with it, he will first check his setup to see if this is sound.

Many smart golfers have a 'routine' to help them get a good setup before they swing. This will have developed over time, possibly with a golf professional's help. Steps in a setup routine might include:
- take your grip whilst holding the club out at waist height
- stand square to the target-line with feet together and ball opposite the middle
- make sure the shoulders are relaxed, and not overly rounded
- move left foot a few inches towards the target
- then move right foot several inches away from target
- possibly splay feet or adjust body to be slightly open or closed
- bend from hips and bring club down to ball, maintaining good posture
- set knee flex to feel comfortable yet 'athletic'
- evenly distribute weight, front to back and side to side
- tilt spine slightly away from target

There is an almost infinite variety of problems that can be caused by a poor setup. For example the grip alone is a subject in its own right. Some of the common ones (with possible consequences shown in brackets) are:
- too much grip pressure (causing tension in the arms, inhibiting the 'release')
- not enough hip bend (making the swing 'armsy' and excessively 'up and down')

- feet too wide (difficulty getting 'through the ball')
- ball too far forward ('reaching' or off balance/toppling forward at impact)
- ball too close (feeling 'cramped', probably with an 'out to in' swing path)
- not setting up square to the line (resulting in unwanted 'compensations' and unpredictable results)
- being 'tense', not breathing well (stiff swing, lifting up)
- too relaxed (swing start is jerky, difficult to recover)

From these examples it is clear that getting your setup right is vital for consistent golf. And that it makes perfect sense to get this right *before* making any changes to your swing (or even learning one in the first place). Partly for this reason I recommend that players see a golf professional to have their 'fundamentals' checked out from time to time.

Another enemy of consistent golf is variable posture. By this I mean the extent to which your body can one day look athletic, yet the next appear somewhat slumped. This change can also happen during the course of a day. I expect we have all seen golfers head to the first tee looking physically perky, only to return at the end of their round looking like they are ready to drop.

Not surprisingly, a golfer's swing will be different in these two states. If you go to the range on one day and all is fine, but the next you really struggle, this could be the reason. If your posture varies from day to day then you are bound to swing differently from day to day too. There is not much that can be done about this apart from trying to get as close as possible to good posture before you start each swing.

I should stress at this point that a large number of golfers don't need to consider posture at all. Many are blessed with a natural good physique. Some look a bit like natural athletes (and many are of course former sportsmen). These lucky few tend to have good balance, and seem 'grounded' all the time. But others have difficulty.

Unfortunately I'm in the latter camp. Being tall, with a not so strong core, does not help me. I also spend most of my time working at a desk, so my shoulders can be quite rounded on some days. My posture often deteriorates during a round as I get tired. If this happens it's noticeable that I swing less well, and I tend to become more inconsistent no matter what I try.

The important point to note from this discussion is that setup and posture matter a lot, and should be considered *before* the swing. A smart golfer thinks in terms of a sequence: (1) setup/posture and (2) swing.

After a poor shot he'll consider if there might have been a problem with his setup or posture *before* thinking about possible problems with his swing. And when he's working on his swing he makes sure that he's aware of his posture, and that each shot is played from a good setup position.

The smart golfer knows that variations in setup and posture produce variations in the swing, and inevitably result in inconsistent golf.

SMART GOLFER CHECKLIST – SETUP AND POSTURE

- ○ Setup consistently, have a routine
- ○ Be aware that posture can vary
- ○ Regularly check setup and posture
- ○ Note the sequence: (1) setup/posture and (2) swing

DECISION MAKING

Good decision making is at the heart of scoring well. Golfers benefit from having good knowledge of the terrain, a solid rationale for shots, and a clear view of whether and when to be aggressive or conservative.

10.   LOCAL KNOWLEDGE

A smart golfer knows that the better informed he is about a course and its pitfalls, the better his round will be.

By common consensus a typical club member's knowledge of his own course gives him a couple of shots advantage over a guest who has not experienced it before. The more a golfer can understand about a given course, the more he is likely to score well.

This local knowledge consists of anything that would help a golfer to gain advantage and avoid disadvantage. Players accumulate this information as rounds are played, from watching others and by learning from the mistakes they make themselves.

The smart golfer makes an effort to become an expert in any courses he plays regularly. During his rounds he will gradually identify the wide and narrow parts of fairways, the best lines from tees, the location of severe hazards and slopes, and the best angles of approach into greens. He will also note the size, shapes and slopes of the greens, so he can play to the best areas for different pin positions.

To check how good your local knowledge is for a particular course, consider what you'd say to a visitor who was about to play it (and let's assume that you want him to do well!). The information you'd give would most probably cover: what shots work best off the tees, particular areas to avoid, and how to handle difficult greens.

Below is an example of what I might say to someone playing a few holes at one of my regular courses. As you'll see there are quite a few tips here that could help the unwary golfer keep out of trouble, and therefore avoid dropping shots.

"The 1ˢᵗ is fairly straightforward. Aim a bit down to the right to avoid the bunker on the left (which will cost a shot). With your second make sure you have enough club to clear the front bunkers; it's uphill. But if the flag is at the back or to one side, don't over-do it because you can easily end up in the thick bushes.

The 2ⁿᵈ is a difficult drive. If you can't mange a draw it's probably better to take a 3 wood or hybrid and perhaps play it as a par 5, particularly if there is a left to right wind pushing towards the tall trees and ferns on the right. After this it's fairly straightforward, but the green is tiered and long, so try to put your ball on the same level as the flag.

The 3ʳᵈ has pot bunkers in the middle of the wide fairway that will cost a shot, so check the distance and play either short or long of them. The left side is the best approach line, but the right isn't a problem since you should only be a wedge or 9 iron away.

On the 7ᵗʰ just play to the elbow of the hole, if you try to cut-off the corner, or go too far, you can get into serious trouble, particularly if it's windy. Play the approach shot short on a line with the right half of the green and run the ball down onto the surface. If you want to go direct for the green you'll need to have spin to hold it (noting that down the back or off to the right isn't a good place to be).

The 8th is a tough uphill par 3 that needs an extra club and a half. The best line is the left half of the green. Anything just off the left hand side will probably come back onto the surface. As long as you are straight it's fine, even towards the back. But anything pin-high and to the right could end up in trouble.

From the 9th tee it is best to aim a bit left. The trees up the right are a nightmare and the wind might push you into them. The bunker on the left isn't too penal and even the semi to the left of it is perfectly ok. With a great drive it may be tempting to go for it in two but you'll need to come in high to hold the surface. Otherwise, either layup to full wedge distance, or play just to the left and beyond the leftmost bunker guarding the green. There's lots of space on that side and from here there is a good line-in for a simple pitch up the length of the green.

Some greens are surrounded by trees and can be shaded and damp (for example the 8th), so putts here can be quite slow. But the greens on holes 7 and 9 can be disproportionately fast because they're raised up and exposed to the wind. Note also that there are severe slopes on sections of the majority of greens. If they're running fast beware. Downhill three putts are not unusual."

As you can see these notes contain quite a bit of information despite only covering part of the round, and even then only with a casual conversation upfront.

Playing with the guest golfer there would be much more to say as we went around the course depending on the player's skill level, the weather conditions, where he was playing his shot from, and the tee and pin positions on the day. Therefore local knowledge can be quite substantial, and can clearly make a difference.

The average golfer might take many rounds to get to grips with a tricky course. If no special effort is made it is surprising how little knowledge sticks in the mind. Whilst playing we tend to have no immediate need for this information.

If we've missed a fairway or green our minds automatically focus on the challenge we're left with, not with checking to see what might have caught us out. And if we've hit the fairway or green there's no need to look elsewhere anyway!

A good way to better understand the terrain of a course, and its ability to fool you, is to look at the holes back-to-front. This 'trick' was once demonstrated to me by a pro who took me in a golf cart around a course in reverse, starting at the 18th green and finishing with the 1st tee. At the time I knew this course quite well and I still remember being taken aback by the amount I learnt from the exercise.

I saw that some of the approach slopes were far more severe than I had thought (*so that's why I often misjudged things*), and that some of the approach angles were greater than they seemed when approaching from far out (*I must remember to layup on the far side in the future*). The elevation changes, both up and down, were also more severe (*so that's why I over or under-cooked it half the time*).

72

During the trip we also examined the greens and surrounds. I could see that some were far more irregular in shape than I had imagined (*so that's why I missed the green quite often on one side*). Also that some of the greenside bunkers were far more extensive than I had realised (*so that's the reason why I and others often end-up in them*).

If you think that better knowledge about your course might help your game then it might be worth making the effort to improve the situation. If you can, do the 'back to front trip' around your home course in a golf cart. Or during a friendly round when you are not pressed for time, look around more than usual. Examine some of the greens and surrounds, and make a point of looking back from landing areas and greens to see if things match-up with what you already have in your head.

Another point to note is that course designers often set out to fool the casual golfer. Course design is a subject in its own right, but the following are examples of common tricks that you might see on the courses that you play:

1. *Twin Bunker Illusion*. The designer makes two bunkers look the same size from a distance, where one is large, and the other small. This is achieved either by designing in proportion (build the small one nearer, and the larger one further away) or by just showing a small lip of the larger one above the ground (so it looks identical in size/shape to the smaller one). More balls end up in these bunkers as a result.

2. *Dead Ground Illusion.* The designer creates a bunker or bunkers so that their top-lips give the impression of being close to the green (when in fact they are 20 – 30 yards away, with 'hidden ground' in-between). This has the effect of making the green appear nearer than it really is – another name for this is foreshortening. Many players will come up short as a result.

3. *Green Shape Illusion.* The designer uses a combination of slope and shape to: make a green appear circular from eye level on the fairway (when in fact it is oval in shape); or make a green appear 'square on' to the fairway (when in fact it is slanted at an angle). Many golfers will either miss the green (thinking it extends when it doesn't), or possibly end up a long way from the pin.

So the smart golfer does everything he can to understand the challenges a course presents, and looks out for designers' attempts to trick the eye.

When playing a new course he'll see if he can get some helpful knowledge beforehand. Some clubs have information like this on the course planner or club website. If he doesn't have any information in advance, he might have a chat with the pro or one of the assistants in the shop, asking about the greens and what he should most watch out for elsewhere on the course.

The smart golfer knows that the better informed he is about a course and its pitfalls, the better his round will be.

SMART GOLFER CHECKLIST – LOCAL KNOWLEDGE

O Become an expert in frequently played courses
O Look 'back to front' to see what can be learned
O Watch out for course designer illusions
O Research and ask someone before playing a new course

11.   RISKY SHOTS

A smart golfer considers the relative merits of a risky shot, against the possibility of failure and the option of a safer alternative.

Making sound choices is a hallmark of the smart golfer. An understanding of probabilities, and a good appreciation of the consequences of both success and failure, are important ingredients in deciding what shot to play.

When facing key decisions, many golfers are repeatedly over-optimistic. They only see positive outcomes and the possibility of failure gets too easily dismissed. Being positive and optimistic is a good mind-set to have over the ball as you start your swing. But before deciding what shot to play it is important to be dispassionate about the alternatives.

Even balanced and rational players can have a problem with this sometimes. For example, a golfer might be upset about his last shot or the result on the last hole. Or things might have gone exceptionally well on the last few holes and you might be on a roll. It is easy to get carried away in this situation.

When asked what they think their chances are with a risky shot, many golfers will say something vague like: *pretty good, reasonable* or *OK*. If optimism takes-over, a basic *OK* can easily turn into *good* and before you know it you are ready to pull the trigger, despite the fact that a safer play is the better option.

For any shot that's at all risky, the smart golfer tries to quantify the chances of success. 'Putting a number on it' helps with being rational.

One method of working out the rough probability is to stand behind the ball and imagine you have to play the shot four times. With how many of these shots would you be successful?

The answer will presumably not be four or zero since this shot is neither a certainty (or you'd not be debating it) nor impossible (or it wouldn't be an option). So you should arrive at one of the following:
- between three and four (i.e. a chance of success greater than 75%)
- three in four (i.e. 75%)
- between two and three (i.e. between 50% and 75%)
- two (i.e. 50%) or
- less than two (i.e. less than 50%)

The higher the number the more it makes sense to take the shot on, and vice versa. With this method you now have a rough estimate of the probability of success and can more readily decide if you need to consider other options.

There is also a further benefit to calculating the odds beforehand. Many golfers get quite upset if they take on a risky shot and it doesn't come off. *Why did I take that shot on?* is a common cry.

Being armed with a 'pre-shot probability' makes it easier for a golfer to accept the outcome, whatever happens.

For example, if you've assessed the odds as 50:50, then by definition this is a somewhat aggressive play. The picture in your mind should be that on average you will make the shot with only two of the four-balls. If the risky-shot doesn't work out there is now a rational reason for it. Since you know this shot will on average only work half of the time, you will hopefully be less likely to pin the blame for a poor outcome on poor execution, bad judgement, or bad luck.

But it's not just about 'making-it' or 'not making-it'. It's also about the possible benefit (of 'making-it') and the possible cost (of 'not making-it'). Therefore as you think through a shot, it makes sense to consider what might happen if the shot works, and perhaps more importantly, what the consequences might be if it doesn't.

In some situations understanding the downside is straightforward, for example if you are facing a water shot you will either make it across, or you won't. If you have to reload it is two shots lost.

But consider an example where you are in trouble and trying to come out with a full shot through a gap in the trees. Anything could happen. You could get through and to the green, or you might only get halfway there. Halfway might be fine (on the fairway), or not so fine (in a pot bunker 50 yards out). Or you might remain in the trees and be left with a similar shot again. In the worst case you might ricochet further into the undergrowth and need a penalty drop.

In a situation like this a touring professional consults with his caddy. Firstly he clarifies what the safe option is, and uses the likely score for this as his baseline. Next he considers the odds for a successful shot. Then he compares the possible benefits of a positive outcome against the costs of a negative one. Golf professionals take the time to do this for a reason. They know that, on average, the more they get decisions like this right, the better they will score.

Clearly a detailed process is too time consuming for amateur golfers during regular play. But one or two (serious) golfers I know do something similar after a round to back-check on marginal decisions. They do this to assess if they got the decision right in the first place, and to learn from it if they didn't.

Unfortunately there isn't a standard way of swiftly reaching a calculated decision on the golf course. But the 'four-balls method' allows you to readily assess your chances. If they are good (say, three in four) then you could simply 'go for it'.

Although this approach might seem a bit crude (since it doesn't consider consequences fully), it works surprisingly well in most circumstances. The important thing is to assess the situation and options as best you can in the time you have.

The experienced player looks out for key factors that could affect the decision one way or another. Here are some example criteria for three of the most common dilemmas we all face on the course. The items marked (+) make the shot more attractive, whilst the items marked (−) should encourage the golfer to look for a safer option.

(+) LONG SHOT TO A GREEN   *(–) LONG SHOT TO A GREEN*

(+) Long Shot to a Green	(–) Long Shot to a Green
No wind	Wind against
Great lie, no slopes	Poor lie and/or difficult slope
Good shot accuracy on the day	Poor shot accuracy on the day
Good fit to club-yardage	Poor fit to club-yardage
Straightforward green	Well-guarded green
Friendly pin position	Difficult pin position
Strong short game	Weak short game
No easy/good layup option	Good layup option

(+) OVER THE WATER   *(–) OVER THE WATER*

(+) Over the Water	(–) Over the Water
Comfortable distance	At limits
No wind, or favourable	Strong wind, particularly against
Good ball striking day	Poor ball striking day
Great lie	Poor lie or downslope
Small layup area	Big layup area, no trouble
Layup still leaves a long carry	Distance from layup point is good

(+) OUT OF THE TREES   *(–) OUT OF THE TREES*

(+) Out of the Trees	(–) Out of the Trees
Big gap	Small gap
Thin foliage	Heavy branches and trunks
Full swing possible	Restricted swing
Fairway between trees and green	Hazards between trees and green
Difficult or backwards chip out	Easy chip out to a good spot

After choosing an option, one way or the other, the smart golfer does everything he can to make sure that he commits to the shot, no matter how close the decision was. Committing to play a safe shot can be difficult for some, whilst taking a risk can be a big deal for others.

The smart golfer is aware of this pitfall. He knows that he needs to approach each and every shot with a positive attitude, or a poor result might follow. If you have made a clear decision to do something, and it's for the right reasons, then it is worth your full attention and focus.

I often see good golfers playing poor layup shots when they really wanted to go for the green, perhaps because they weren't emotionally committed to the shot. But it might also be that with a layup shot there often isn't an obvious target to aim for, and the golfer is merely thinking, *OK, all I need to do is just push the ball forward about 100 yards.*

As a result they don't take aim properly and sometimes end-up making a half-hearted swing at it. To make matters worse if they execute this shot badly there is a good chance that they will make a mental note not to layup next time, even though it was the right decision in the first place!

The smart golfer considers the relative merits of a risky shot, against the possibility of failure and the option of a safer alternative.

SMART GOLFER CHECKLIST – RISKY SHOTS

- O Understand the chances of making/not making a shot
- O 'Put a number on it', perhaps use 'three in four' to help
- O Consider the benefit of 'making it' (against safe option)
- O Consider the cost of 'not making it' (against safe option)
- O Use the odds to rationally accept bad outcomes
- O Know key (+) and (–) factors for common situations
- O Positively commit to safety shots, with good focus

12.   *AGGRESSIVE OR CONSERVATIVE?*

A smart golfer has clear objectives and flexes his playing style to get the best result.

When considering a shot from the trees, if there is a gap, some golfers automatically choose to 'go for it'. Yet others nearly always just chip out sideways. By taking on the risk, the former golfer will often lose more shots than he gains. But the latter golfer will perhaps miss some opportunities. Which is right?

The first thing to note is that a smart golfer is focused on scoring the best he can. The ambition and ultimate goal of a club golfer is likely to be to get his handicap down to the lowest number possible. After all, this is the indisputable measure of a player's standard. Someone with a handicap in the 20s might look longingly at those who play comfortably off 18. And those who make it to single figures get respect from all.

So let's assume that your goal is to score better or to get your handicap down to the lowest possible level. What strategy do you employ to achieve this? Is it to play safe all the time, or should you generally go for it?

Let's consider two golfers of the same standard where one tends to play safe whilst the other is more of a risk-taker. Our conservative player would perhaps: take the safe line off the tee;

always layup if there is any doubt about the shot; always aim for the centre of the green; and never take a risk with a recovery shot. The aggressive player might also play some safe shots, but he'll tend to go for it most of the time.

The first of these players is in some ways playing smart because he doesn't make many mistakes. He is unlikely to get a birdie but at the same time probably doesn't make many double or triple-bogeys either. Many golfers would accuse this man of missing quite a bit of the fun element in golf. But if he is content, it is hard to say that there is anything wrong with this approach.

On the other hand the second player is likely to get some birdies here and there, and possibly even an eagle from time to time. But he is equally likely to have more disasters and his overall score will be blighted with some big numbers. But if he is happy with this there isn't a problem, is there?

The first golfer gets his contentment from steadily plotting his way around the course and not dropping shots needlessly. He will be fairly consistent and will on average outscore the second player in stroke play.

The second golfer will shoot a mixture of high and low scores. He is probably more focused on the 'high spots' in his round – for example where he hit an incredible drive or approach shot, or made a brilliant recovery shot from an almost impossible situation.

Let's consider how these two golfers would do in match play. The first is likely to be 'in' each hole, not giving much away. The second will lose some holes by a margin (because he's in trouble), but is equally likely to win others outright (when his shots come off).

In fact these two golfers would make a strong pairing in pairs match play. The opposition would have to contend with not being given many holes whilst at the same time facing some good one-off scores too.

In the same way that our two golfers might combine to good effect, the smart golfer flexes his style to get the best possible outcome. On some holes and with some shots he will play safe, yet on others he'll take the option that appears more adventurous. The style he adopts will depend on the nature of the round and the particular situation he faces with each shot.

The smart golfer knows that *the risk of losing a shot or two generally outweighs the chance to gain a possible shot*. Therefore in stroke play the smart golfer is more focused on avoiding trouble than in seeking to pull off a risky shot. This point is vital to scoring well.

In singles match play our smart golfer might adopt a similar conservative approach. By delivering good scores hole after hole, and appearing consistent, he will be able to apply steady pressure to his opponent. But if he sees that he's about to lose a hole or the match unless he does something special, he'll go ahead and take a risk.

In pairs match play our smart golfer will decide based on the likely score the opposition will get, and what he expects his partner to deliver on the hole concerned. For example, if his partner is likely to get a safe bogey, he might as well make an attempt to get a par. This is an example where a shot can be considered to be a 'shot to nothing' – if he messes-up there is no real cost.

Shots to nothing also crop up regularly in Stableford golf. If you are heading for a net double bogey then you might as well go for it with a risky approach shot or a long putt. A net double bogey counts the same as a triple or a quad (whereas a single net bogey gets a point on the card).

Similarly in eclectic competitions* golfers often throw all caution to the wind if there is a chance of getting a birdie. If you already have a par or net par in the bag in the overall competition, then there is little point in playing safe at the same hole every time (though this has to be balanced with the possibility of winning the individual competition on the day).

Incidentally, many players always shoot at flags, though in my view this is a questionable practice for the average golfer. Even though they might not consider this to be an aggressive play, it often is. Unless you play to a high standard, or are exceptionally strong with approach shots and your short game, it is usually best to aim at the centre of the green.

....

* An eclectic competition is a multi-round tournament typically run over a period of months. For example one of my local clubs runs a 'summer eclectic competition' on a weekday afternoon over a period of 12 weeks. Each player registers his gross scores by hole. At the end of the period, a cumulative low gross score over 18 holes is calculated for each player containing their best scores on each hole. Prizes are given for the best gross and net totals.

On average more shots are lost than are gained by shooting directly at pins. For the vast majority of golfers, *the middle of the green is nearly always good.*

Irrespective of whether you tend to play conservatively or aggressively overall, an optimum playing strategy certainly includes taking a risk to:
- get a Stableford point
- improve your overall eclectic score
- give yourself a chance of halving or winning a hole
- or to 'better' your partner if he is 'safe' in match play

So is it right to play conservatively or aggressively as an overall strategy? Phil Mickelson and Luke Donald are both successful golfers, yet the former is 'aggressive' and the latter 'conservative'. Phil has won several majors, but to date has yet to reach World Number 1 in the rankings. In contrast, Luke has been World Number 1 for over a year, but is yet to win a major.

So how you play is clearly a matter of personal choice. It comes down to your ambitions, your abilities and what makes you happy.

I know quite a few golfers who say, *I don't like making mistakes, I get good results by taking the safe route and I manage the occasional birdie anyway.* Provided these players are happy with their scoring or handicaps, then there seems no reason to change.

But I can also relate to golfers who say, *part of the reason I play the game is to take on difficult shots, so I'll continue to do this even if it's not optimum.* These golfers certainly seem to have fun, or at least experience more highs (albeit with lows mixed-in).

This aggressive approach also seems fine provided the golfers concerned are content with their scores and handicaps. If so you might say that these players have decided that 'repeated risk taking' is part of their overall happiness equation.

It is possible to do well with both approaches. But it seems to me that, whatever your default approach, it helps to remain flexible and to be prepared to change as required.

The smart golfer has clear objectives and flexes his playing style to get the best result.

SMART GOLFER CHECKLIST – AGGRESSIVE/CONSERVATIVE

- O   Have clear objectives for rounds
- O   Middle of the green is nearly always good
- O   Generally flex style towards safety in stroke play
- O   Take risks in match play as required

HANDLING TROUBLE

A key aspect of golf is being able to deal with adversity. Heavy rough, trees, fairway bunkers and other hazards await players en route to the green. Despite facing these challenges frequently, many golfers still don't handle trouble well.

13.   LOST BALL?

A smart golfer is expert at finding his ball, and doesn't hesitate to play a provisional.

Every golfer hits the ball off line from time to time. But the smart golfer handles this better than most. For example, he tends to have better than average skills at finding his ball.

After hitting a shot offline, instead of trudging off in anger, a smart golfer does two things. Firstly, assuming he saw the result, he notes where the ball disappeared. To help with memorising this he will often state the location out loud. For example he might say, *it went in between the third and fourth bush* or, *I think it's on a line with the right edge of the tall tree.*

If he is at all unsure of where the ball went, he engages his playing partners to either agree or disagree with his statement. He tries to get their views whilst the shot is still fresh in their minds, and in any case before leaving the tee.

Having got the best sense of the ball's line, the smart golfer then considers how far the ball travelled. Distance can be just as important as line, particularly when searching for a ball in heavy rough. It is important to focus the search on the most likely area, and the more accurate you can be with your assessment of where the ball was lost, the better.

For example, you might estimate that a wayward drive went about 200 yards. It therefore makes sense to go this distance, as close as possible to the line of flight, and park your bag or golf cart there (as a reference for the search). Getting to the right spot should be straightforward if you have a GPS. Many units have a 'mark distance' feature which will count up to the required number as you walk.

If you don't have a GPS, or you've lost track of how far you are from the tee, consider what you do know. *Where would a normal drive finish on the fairway on this hole? Where are your playing partners' balls? How long is the hole, and how far is it to the green?* Anything that can help focus the search will increase your chances of finding the ball.

These measures might seem a bit over the top, but there is a two-shot penalty at stake here. So even roughly approximating the distance the ball travelled can be helpful, particularly if you are unfamiliar with the course. I often see visiting four-balls spread out across an area of 50 or even 60 yards, searching in heavy rough. It is obvious that a good proportion of their time is being completely wasted since they can't all be looking in the right area!

Smart golfers make a point of marking their balls with a marker-pen so they can be uniquely identified. This only takes a few seconds. Many golfers just don't do this because they feel it is something for top golfers only (which is not true), or that it's too much bother (which is not true either).

The rules of golf are clear – you have to be certain that a ball is yours, otherwise it is deemed not to be. It is easy to forget the number on a ball, and whilst the likelihood of finding another ball of the same brand and model is small, it does happen. I recently witnessed a pair of golfers losing a hole for just this reason. They were not amused, particularly since it was in a semi final club knockout competition and lost by one hole!

Putting a large mark on the ball, for example your initials in big letters, is helpful for some. Walking up the fairway to a group's drives it is easy to spot the one with lots of ink on it. This can save a bit of time, avoid confusion, and perhaps help a senior golfer who prefers not to stoop down too often.

Any time you think your ball might be lost, it is best to play 'a provisional'. There are two reasons for this. Firstly, if it is lost, you will have another ball in play and can carry on without walking back (without embarrassment or loss of time). Secondly, if the problem was a bad swing, the second attempt gives you a chance to get this out of your system.

Many golfers just don't bother to play a provisional ball, or they don't do it well. One reason for this is that some playing partners make it hard for errant golfers to play a provisional. They either press on without thinking, or do so as part of 'gamesmanship'. If this happens just say clearly *I'm sorry, but I'd like to play a provisional, if that's alright?* Since it is your right to do so, they can't really complain.

If you play a second ball, it is important to do this properly. This means going through your normal routine, committing to the shot, and taking dead aim again. If you don't do this, and perhaps rush, the result may even be worse. I see this time and time again and it is not a pretty sight.

The smart golfer is wise to this. If there is any risk of not finding his ball, he plays a provisional and is good at it. He takes his time and doesn't get embarrassed about holding up his playing partners. By doing this he will be well rehearsed for the day when he really needs a good second ball in play. The objective is to make playing a second ball 'just routine'. If you can learn to take a provisional as a matter of course, and do this well, it will stand you in good stead.

Finally, there are a couple of rules that are relevant here.

Firstly, remember to 'declare' the provisional ball by stating *this is a provisional*. And check that your playing partners have heard this too. Many a golfer has fallen foul of not saying anything, or saying it but others not hearing it. When this happens the rules force the second ball to be the one 'in play' and you will be 'three off the tee' even if you subsequently find your first one.

Secondly, here is a (rules) tip that I learnt from a smart golfer a year or so ago that I have found really helpful, particularly since I'm quite wayward. The rules say you have *five minutes from the start of the search*. The smart golfer knows this and will often hang back (or at least not charge on) until his playing partners are available to help him with the search.

So if it's not too disruptive, or if finding your ball is critical to your score or match, wait until your playing partners are free to help before moving into the search area. Four golfers searching for the whole five minutes is in effect 20 minutes search time. This way you are several times more likely to find a problem-ball when compared to initially searching on your own!

The smart golfer is expert at finding his ball, and doesn't hesitate to play a provisional.

SMART GOLFER CHECKLIST – LOST BALL?

- Memorise and state 'out loud' the line of the ball
- Estimate the probable distance travelled
- Centre the search on the intersection of line and distance
- Park golf bag or cart close to the spot
- Ensure balls are uniquely marked with a marker-pen
- Always play a 'provisional', and do this well
- Remember to say out loud *playing a provisional*
- At critical times, wait for others before searching

14. *FAIRWAY BUNKERS*

A smart golfer handles fairway bunkers well, and plays recovery shots with the correct club.

Fairway bunkers can be a real pain, particularly when playing an unfamiliar course. You've hit a great drive, but it has just leaked a bit to the right at the end, and rolled into a trap.

As you reach the ball, the first task is to examine the lie. If it is sitting down, the arc of the swing will make contact with the sand first, and a normal full shot will not be possible. This can be frustrating, but it is important to 'not deny the lie'. The absolute priority must be to get the ball out, and back onto the fairway.

In most cases a traditional greenside bunker 'splash shot' will be required where the club strikes the sand first and there is no direct contact with the ball. In bunkers where there is any significant lip, a sand wedge will be required.

But in a shallow bunker, it might be feasible to use a straighter-faced club, like an 8 iron. This still won't make a completely clean contact, but it might be possible to nudge the ball 40 yards or so up the fairway.

If you are lucky, the ball will be sitting up and it will be possible to get a club cleanly into the back of the ball. Provided the lip is not a problem, and your stance is on a fairly flat part of the bunker, a more conventional shot is now possible, albeit with some adjustments such as:

- playing the ball back in the stance (to reduce the chance of sand getting caught between club and ball)
- digging the feet into the sand (to get a firm 'base' for the swing)
- gripping down on the club (to compensate for the feet being dug in)

To reduce the risk of slipping underfoot, it is usually best to take at least one more club and to play only a three-quarter shot. It is better to make a solid partial-swing, making clean contact, than it is to risk slipping or catching the sand before the ball (bearing in mind that your feet are on a questionable surface).

With a good lie and little or no lip, the smart golfer won't hesitate to use a hybrid or fairway wood. The flat base of these clubs handles the sand surface really well provided you can get properly into the back of the ball.

This all seems fairly straightforward, but what if it is a close call whether the ball can be picked off the sand cleanly or not? Faced with this problem, the smart golfer thinks through the consequences of making a mess of the shot. If the likely result is only the same as for a splash shot, then it is acceptable to take the shot on. But the last thing you need is to be in a worse position than before.

Another dilemma might occur when there is a good lie in the bunker but it is marginal whether a shot will catch the lip or not.

In this case there are several more things to consider. It is a question of geometry.

Firstly there is the angle from the ball to clear the lip. Secondly there are possible 'slope' effects – the ball could be on an upslope (making it easier to clear the lip), or a downslope (making it more difficult). Thirdly it makes sense to allow an extra margin for clearance, since shots from sand can sometimes come out low (and there are no prizes for catching the lip!).

All too often golfers are overly optimistic in these situations. If you are at all doubtful it makes sense to step away and ask: *would I easily clear that lip 75% of the time*? If not, think again.

After the decision it is important to properly commit to the shot. If there is any chance of catching the lip, take a higher lofted club, or revert to playing a splash shot, and just move on calmly.

Despite thinking things through, all golfers will from time to time be about to play a shot and realise that they don't have enough loft to be certain of clearing the lip. In this situation it is tempting to carry on, particularly if there is time pressure. If you have already taken some time over the shot, you almost seem obliged to.

The smart golfer knows that just playing the shot isn't the right thing to do and acts on this. He walks back to his bag saying clearly, *I'm sorry I can't get out with this club*. Speaking up in this way is quite powerful. Any reasonable person will not want to force you to play a club that you can't get out with. For one thing they might have to watch you do it all over again!

If the shot is from a particularly deep bunker, where you need to clamber down, it can be helpful to take an additional club or two in with you in the first place, to cover all possibilities. Incidentally, the rules allow you to lay extra clubs on the sand in a bunker, provided that you do not improve the lie of the ball or test the condition of the hazard.

Walking to your ball with more than one club in hand, or being prepared to go back to your bag if your chosen club turns out to be not quite right, is an approach that applies elsewhere too, for example in the rough or the trees.

Sometimes you will realise before you play that you can't get out with the club in hand. Other times you might be able to get out, but realise that another club would do a better job. In both cases the smart golfer knows what to do.

The smart golfer handles fairway bunkers well, and plays recovery shots with the correct club.

SMART GOLFER CHECKLIST – FAIRWAY BUNKERS

- In fairway bunkers, examine the lie first
- If in doubt, play the safer shot
- Watch for downslopes affecting the escape angle
- Take one less club (more loft) for safety
- Always use the optimum club for recovery shots
- Go back and get another club if needs be

15.   ROUGH AND TREES

A smart golfer handles the rough and trees both sensibly and well.

No matter how straight you are, from time to time you'll find yourself in heavy rough. The task now is to get safely back onto the fairway and out of trouble.

There are two problems with long grass. Firstly, there is the danger that the grass will affect either your backswing or downswing, so you won't be able to cleanly contact the back of the ball. The grass might either slow your club-head down before it reaches the ball, reducing the power at impact, or in the worst case wrap around the hosel, closing the clubface and smothering the ball (and perhaps stopping the swing altogether).

Even if you manage to maintain good club-head speed, it is likely that some grass will be caught between clubface and ball, so the impact will be 'scruffy' at best. In order to prevent this, a more vertical approach might help. So consider a steeper swing, with a sort of 'chopping' action. 'Gripping down' can also help.

Secondly, even if a good contact is possible, the height and thickness of the grass in front of the ball might prevent it from getting airborne as it tries to take-off. Even with the loft of a sand wedge, it might still not be possible to get out.

With all these considerations it makes sense to get a feel for the shot beforehand, by taking a couple of practice swings in similar grass nearby. If you are confident you can get cleanly enough into the back of the ball, with enough power and loft on the clubface, then fine. Otherwise, think again. There is nothing worse than thrashing away in heavy rough and failing to get out altogether.

Quite often it won't be possible to play towards the green or back to the fairway because the grass will prevent this. But sometimes the ball will be lying in such a way that good contact can be made to play the ball in another direction. The smart golfer weighs up this option. For example, it is often possible to get the ball onto a parallel fairway, leaving a reasonable shot to follow.

The alternative is to seek a drop under penalty of one shot. If there is a good area within two club lengths (not nearer the hole) then take this option. If not, consider the option to drop back on a line with the flag (or in the worst case go back to the tee). On many occasions I have found a track or path cutting through the rough that isn't immediately apparent from the search area. This can turn out quite well, particularly if it enables you to make a full swing with (say) a fairway wood.

Many golfers just don't consider these options, perhaps because they simply don't think, or feel some embarrassment at the possibility of walking a long way back after all the effort of finding the ball in the first place. But from deep rough, 'dropping back' is often the best option.

Trees and bushes present a different type of problem. If there is any kind of obstruction, or if an unhindered swing is not possible, then consider the options, and choose the one that you feel most comfortable with (see also Chapter 11 – Risky Shots).

Having chosen, the shot itself still deserves proper consideration. There might be options to go more, or less, towards the hole. These options might in turn have a lesser, or greater, chance of clearing the trees on the way out, and the areas that the ball will land (or roll to) might also present different levels of risk.

Before taking the shot, it makes sense to walk out of the trees in the direction of the intended line of play, and to take a look around. From the undergrowth it might appear a simple job to play through a gap, but the outside view could tell a different story. For example the overhang might be more extensive than it appears from the inside. Similarly, playing in the direction of the flag might be an obvious choice, but are there bunkers or other obstacles on that line?

Walking out and looking around pre-shot also helps prevent another common error, namely 'coming out too well'. I regularly see golfers playing what seems to be a great recovery shot, only for the ball to run though the fairway into a bunker, rough or trees on the other side. A key point to remember is that a recovery shot is not just *what line?*, but also *what distance?*

Once all this is clear, it is a good idea to step away and rehearse the swing nearby, particularly if the situation requires a contrived-shot. Having gone to the trouble of working out the optimum shot, it doesn't make sense to risk it because this is the first and only time you've ever attempted this particular contortion!

The most common shot required from the trees is a low shot, possibly hugging the ground, in order to get under the overhanging branches. I regularly spend time practising this type of shot. In my case this has been a great help since the trees and I are old friends!

The next time you are at the range with a few balls left over, why not hit a few shots like this? Set the ball back, open-up your stance a bit, and swing away. The ability to accurately and cleanly hit a low shot is a great tool to have in your armoury.

The smart golfer handles the rough and trees both sensibly and well.

SMART GOLFER CHECKLIST – ROUGH AND TREES

○ Examine the height of grass in front and behind the ball
○ In heavy rough, examine the alternatives
○ Consider playing sideways, e.g. to another fairway
○ Look for paths and tracks 'back on a line'
○ Walk out of trees and look around before playing the shot
○ A recovery shot is both line *and* distance
○ Rehearse before playing from rough and trees
○ Practise low shots with spare balls at the range

16.   NO PROBLEM

A smart golfer is expert at avoiding trouble, and accomplished at dealing with it.

The first principle of handling trouble is to avoid it altogether. So every now and then it pays to consider if there is more you can do to achieve this. For your home course consider the following questions:

- *Are there some bunkers that you visit more than others?*
- *On some holes do you frequently visit certain areas of rough or trees?*
- *Are there places where you regularly get blocked out?*
- *Are there certain holes where the approach angle makes all the difference?*

Simply going through these questions, hole by hole, might flag up some possibilities of what you could do differently to avoid trouble. As you think it through also consider what others do differently to avoid these problems. If you think some players might be 'smarter' than you are at navigating around the course, it makes sense to learn from them.

A classic situation where some golfers can benefit from alternative thinking is on long par 4s and shorter par 5s, where it is sometimes smart to be less ambitious with the second shot. After a good tee shot, being left with a shot of around 220 yards, many golfers automatically reach for their 3 woods to move the ball forwards as far as possible. But even if they are straight they usually won't get there, and will typically be left with an awkward 'partial shot'.

Holes are often designed to catch out wayward shots that come up short in the zone 30 – 60 yards out. I can think of many examples of holes like this on the courses I play. They are set up so that anything wayward in this range will be severely punished (whereas short or long of this distance range is fine).

When faced with this situation, a sound alternative is to play (say) two 9 irons instead. This approach might reduce the chances of a par, but it will also considerably decrease the chances of a double bogey. The smart golfer looks out for holes like these, and alters his game accordingly.

Irrespective of how good we are at avoiding them, in a typical round most golfers inevitably pay several visits to fairway bunkers, trees or the rough. Once in trouble, it is often the case that recovery shots are not executed well. This is no coincidence. The only time most golfers play shots like these in anger, is on the course.

But the smart golfer makes a point of being accomplished at recovery shots.

Practising from fairway bunkers can be a great help if you visit them often, or if you particularly struggle when you do. From time to time it helps to place a few balls in a fairway bunker, playing shots from a variety of lies. Observe the angle of flight for different clubs from different lies to get a sense of the trajectory and distance compared to normal.

For shots where the lip interferes, double check your lie to see if direct contact is possible, definitely not possible, or whether it's a 'maybe'. After this assess the underfoot slope to determine the angle needed for clearance. For a given lip perhaps try different clubs to get a clear sense of what is required to escape cleanly.

If you regularly play wooded courses, there is much to be gained by improving your ability to escape from the trees. One player I know does this by regularly hitting low shots at the range.

He aims at targets 50 to 200 yards away and plays shots with a 4 iron, hybrid, 3 wood and driver, to simulate being in the trees. He sets himself the challenge of keeping the flight of the ball below head height. Unsurprisingly, in competitive rounds he hits some pretty amazing shots from what seem like very bad situations. This definitely bolsters his game, particularly in match play situations.

There isn't much that can be done to prepare for heavy rough other than by dropping a few balls in bad situations, and learning what you can from this. But even a handful of shots can help with the assessment of what is and is not possible. Particularly in late spring, when the rough suddenly comes up, I see golfers failing to get out with their shots from 'the long stuff' (yet by late summer it doesn't seem to be a problem).

Improving your ability from all of these situations can help your score. So smart golfers practise recovery shots. They learn the basics well, and keep these topped-up. If needs be, consider some help with technique from a golf professional, for example to master shots from fairway bunkers and rough.

Now might also be a good time to consider your overall attitude to trouble. You have probably heard the expression 'take the pain' before. But I would like to give this a bit more attention because the logic behind it is so compelling. When smart players experience trouble they don't let it ruffle them, even if they end up with a very bad score on one hole. They just seem to treat it 'matter-of-factly' and carry on regardless.

One key to this is not denying the odds. For example, if you are in heavy rough and it is improbable that you'll get safely onto the fairway, but there is a reasonable drop option, it is usually right to just take the drop. Moving on from a bad situation in a good mental state is absolutely fine.

Excluding a lost ball or 'finding the water', golfers tend to find the most common cause of double and triple bogeys are compound errors, where a failed recovery shot lands the player in similar, or worse, trouble. A bad episode like this can even upset a player so much that it destroys a round. So it makes sense to avoid this happening at all costs.

That is why 'taking the pain and moving on' is such a compelling strategy.

The smart golfer is expert at avoiding trouble, and accomplished at dealing with it.

SMART GOLFER CHECKLIST – NO PROBLEM

O Make every effort to avoid trouble in the first place
O Identify frequently occurring problem situations
O Think through alternatives
O Learn from other players
O Consider the 2x 9 iron approach on long par 4s
O Practise from fairway bunkers and rough
O Practise shots below head height
O Don't deny the odds
O When required, take the pain and move on

LONG GAME
IMPROVEMENT

Most players would be hard pressed to describe their performance from tee to green other than to say how well they struck the ball. This is missing a trick. In order to reach their potential, players need to understand all the factors that impact how well they score, and to note that much of the challenge in golf comes before you swing the club.

17.   GOOD, AVERAGE OR POOR

A smart golfer routinely assesses his performance from tee to green, and is therefore able to easily see the problems that most affect his game.

Smart golfers not only try to take the best decisions on the golf course, but also to systematically learn from their mistakes, and thus improve over time.

The average golfer takes roughly 90 shots a round. These would typically comprise about:

- 40 long shots   (from at least 50 yards away from the green)
- 14 short shots   (from within 50 yards of the green)
- 36 putts   (from the fringe or on the green itself)

The more shots you play well, the better you will score, and vice versa. And the more you know about the reasons for a poor or 'less-than-good' shot, the more you will know what to do about it.

After a round I sometimes reflect on my play and note down information about my long shots. The basic idea is to assess each shot as being Good, Average or Poor. In this definition Good means 'happy with the shot', Poor means 'not happy with the shot', and Average means 'not Good, but not Poor either' (in other words 'OK').

Alongside my Poor shots I make a note of anything that might have contributed to this. For example, I might suspect I took the wrong club, was too aggressive, or made a dreadful swing. Similarly, it should be clear if I denied the lie, did not line up correctly, or perhaps didn't get the technique right from a sloping lie.

But other times it is difficult to come up with any reason at all for a Poor shot. In this case the challenge is to become 'more aware', or 'mindful', at the time. So immediately after a Poor shot ask yourself, *what happened there?*, and spend a moment thinking it through.

When I have this problem I look at my divot, consider the ball flight and ask myself questions. *Did I have a clear target? Did I commit to the shot? Was I setup OK? Was that a smooth swing? Did I stay in balance?* I try to at least eliminate some things from the range of possibilities.

As I rate my shots after a round, I also make notes alongside some of my Average shots, particularly if there is a clear reason why it didn't warrant a rating of Good. Poor shots are perhaps more of a priority than Average ones, but it is still helpful to note down any obvious reasons why a shot was Average, as opposed to Good.

Alongside my Good shots I leave most of the entries blank. However, I do make a point of congratulating myself on the 'exceptionally good' ones. I find that deliberately recalling the shots that I am most happy with provides a 'positive memory' that gives me confidence and satisfaction. There is also the argument that if you focus solely on the negative aspects of your game, it might drag you down.

The benefit of routinely assessing your play from tee to green this way starts immediately. For example when I first analysed my rounds over several weeks I could see that:

- my drives from the first tee were appalling (a bad start can be soul-destroying)
- I sometimes forgot to line up properly (this cost me a shot more often than not)
- I was a bit lax on checking lies and slopes (so I often messed up what appeared to be straightforward shots)
- I repeatedly struggled with shots from fairway bunkers (perhaps because I had never practised or properly-learned how to play these)

At this point I should perhaps clarify one aspect about the Good, Average and Poor (GAP) ratings. It is important to separate 'what you did' from 'where the ball ended up'. In other words if you *prepare well for the shot, and put a good swing on it, that is all you can do*, and you should be content with it (even if in some way you are not happy with the result).

For example, it is perfectly possible to play a Good shot where the ball takes nasty bounce and runs into the water, costing a stroke. Similarly, it is possible to hit a Good shot which catches the top of a bunker and ends up 'plugged' (whereas a yard more might have been brilliant).

The reverse is also true. A drive that is hit way offline, but gets a lucky bounce off a tree back onto the fairway, should be classified as a Poor. The same would go for a 5 iron approach shot that finished on the green despite being 'thinned'.

After logging your shots for a few rounds, your most frequent problems should become apparent. You should also be able to identify less-frequent problems that might otherwise have been hard to surface.

Your overall GAP figures should give you a good sense of your play from tee to green for a given round. The Good total will show how many shots you were happy with, and the Poor total should show how many you were definitely not happy with.

On a good ball-striking day you ought to have a high proportion of Good shots. But when your swing is off you will most probably have a high number of Poor ones. Similarly on a day when you are 'mentally sharp' the figures will look better, and on a bad day they will look worse.

You should also find that your score correlates with the number of Poor shots you have in the round (assuming an average day on and around the greens). In other words the higher the number of Poor shots the higher your score, and vice versa. This should provide proof of often-made statement: *it is the bad shots in a round that determine a player's score, not the good ones.*

When I first started looking at my GAP numbers I found on average that about 30% of my long shots were Good, 40% were Average, and 30% were Poor. As the scores for my rounds came down by several shots, my GAP numbers also improved. Within a year or so I had progressed to about 50% Good, 30% Average, and 20% Poor. It was no coincidence that during the same period the number of long shots in my rounds also reduced from around 40 to nearer 36, and my handicap came down by several shots.

By focussing on my Poor shots, and trying to understand the reasons behind these, I was able to more clearly see what was holding me back, and do something about it. At one point I set myself the objective to have a maximum of eight Poor shots in a round. It was perhaps no surprise that I achieved this on the day when I shot my best ever score to date.

From time to time I also found it was useful to just concentrate on the reasons behind my Average shots. In other words I focussed on the problems that caused these shots to be just Average, instead of Good. This helped me to eliminate some of the simple mistakes I made and I found that I began to hit more fairways and greens (instead of semi-rough and fringes).

The GAP approach helped me to sharpen up all sides of my play from tee to green. Whether you use this approach or something similar, I encourage you to be thorough in the assessment of your long game. If you can identify and resolve issues systematically, you should be able to improve over time. As this happens, it is reasonable to expect that your shots per round will also come down too.

The smart golfer routinely assesses his performance from tee to green, and is therefore able to easily see the problems that most affect his game.

SMART GOLFER CHECKLIST – GOOD, AVERAGE OR POOR

○ Systematically assess play from tee to green
○ Exclude luck from individual shot judgements
○ After a Poor or Average shot ask *why?*
○ Remember and re-live exceptionally Good shots
○ Work on the problems that have the most impact
○ Use ratios to track performance and set targets

18.   PRIORITISE AND FOCUS

A smart golfer differentiates between 'Preparation' and 'Execution', and focuses on the problems that have the potential to cost the most shots.

Looking at a list of problems with your shots it should be obvious that many are to do with decisions and actions before the start of the swing, whilst others are solely to do with the swing itself. Problems can therefore be categorised as relating to 'Preparation' or 'Execution'.

Preparation problems tend to arise as a result of some flawed assessment, calculation or decision, or from the failure to setup well. Example Preparation problems might include:
-   getting the distance wrong
-   making the wrong adjustment for wind, elevation or roll
-   forgetting to check for, or not taking account of, slopes and bad lies
-   choosing the wrong shot or target for the situation
-   being overly optimistic
-   not having an aiming point

In some ways it seems logical to assume that we can all get better at the Preparation aspect of the game just by remembering to do it right next time, in other words by being mindful. But when I first started using this approach I found that achieving this in practice was far from easy. Despite my best efforts to always check the obvious things, I still sometimes came off the course having failed to do so.

One reason for this was that I was all too often simply 'not with it', after a tiring day or week at work. If you are mentally tired you won't do some things well, and are equally likely to forget some others altogether.

Another reason was perhaps the fact that I was already a relatively experienced golfer by that time, and I therefore had long-established bad habits. For example, my bad habit of 'not checking things' was part of my long-standing way of playing golf (you could say that not checking lies and slopes was part of my 'routine'!).

But these days I set out to religiously check the basics for each shot before I play (such as lies and slopes), and I am certain that I make fewer errors as a consequence. From time to time I still slip up, but I am usually able to recognise a lapse and then try to make sure it doesn't happen again.

It occurs to me that readers who have not played much golf before have a 'one-time' opportunity regarding Preparation matters. If you start checking the basics now, you will have a better chance of avoiding problems, and should make things easier for yourself in the future. There is no downside to putting sound principles into your game at an early stage.

Execution problems are to do with the physical act of swinging the club and striking the ball. These are very different in nature to Preparation problems, not least because every golfer's swing is in some way unique. To illustrate this point consider just a handful of Execution problems that crop up regularly in my own game:

- lifting up on takeaway
- poor rhythm/swinging too fast
- coming 'over the top' in the downswing
- being too steep into the ball
- trying to 'murder it'

Sometimes I find it difficult to come up with any meaningful observations at all for many shots. But all golfers play a proportion of shots badly and don't have a clue as to why, let alone what to do about it.

The best that can be done here is to think about the problem after the round, or perhaps the following morning. It may be that you still come up blank, but from time to time you might get an inkling, or at least be able to eliminate some of the possible causes.

I find it helps sometimes to mark problems with either a 'P' (for Preparation) or an 'E' (for Execution), and to add up the totals for each. A low number of E's shows that my swing is working well. A low numbers of P's points to me being mentally sharp on a given day. Every now and then, both of these numbers will be low, and I'll be very happy. Equally some days both numbers will be high, and I will have had a terrible day (but that's golf!).

Many Poor shots have both a Preparation and Execution problem element to them. However, looking at shots with these symptoms it is clear that Execution (swing) problems are sometimes caused by preceding Preparation errors, at least in part.

This of course makes sense. If you are uncomfortable with the shot you are about to play, or if you have setup incorrectly, it is not surprising if you make a hash of the swing. There is a sequence here, mental –> physical, or Preparation -> Execution.

When I first realised this I went back over my GAP information, and reviewed it taking account of 'sequence' (in other words allowing for the fact that a pre-swing problem might have affected my swing). I found that my physical play was much better than I'd given myself credit for. In fact it was more like what I achieved on the range.

The information collected about your shots can also be used to find other types of problem that are sometimes difficult to spot. For example golfers can have repeated issues with playing shots:
- from the first tee (e.g. due to nerves or not warming up)
- on certain holes (e.g. on a specific tee or with a specific approach shot)
- with certain clubs (e.g. playing 3 woods off the tee or with long irons generally)
- under certain conditions (e.g. in windy conditions)
- towards the end of a round (e.g. due to tiring)

If you catalogue your shots over a number of rounds, it should be evident if you suffer from some of these issues. When I first did this I could see that:
- my tee shots on two or three holes were consistently very poor (perhaps the holes intimidated me)

- playing in wind was not one of my strengths (and I still find this a challenge)
- driving was one of the weakest parts of my game (though I am thankfully now much better at this)

As you can see from the above, by using Good, Average and Poor ratings, and flagging problems as being related to Preparation or Execution, I had no trouble coming up with a list of things to work on. It is therefore important to prioritise.

An obvious way to do this is to look at your Poor and Average shots and highlight the problems that have the potential to most damage your score. I use the word *potential* because simply focussing on the shots that cost you can be misleading. As we have discussed, a dreadful shot can sometimes cost nothing, whereas a great shot can, in some circumstances, end up costing a stroke or more.

All golfers will score better in the long term if they can eradicate their most inaccurate shots. So flagging any shot that is way off line makes sense, even if on this occasion you didn't end up in trouble or lose a stroke.

Note though that judgements on accuracy should be tempered by the fact that it is far more difficult to hit shots into the wind, or from severe slopes and bad lies, than it is from a good flat lie on a calm day. So don't be too hard on yourself, and make allowances for this.

Another important factor is *how you feel* about a shot. Reading your emotions immediately afterwards can give additional insight. Any shot you are 'appalled with' almost certainly has the potential to cost you a shot or two in other situations, even if it worked out just fine this time. Your own judgement is the most important factor in assessing what should be classified as potentially costly or not.

As you examine your rounds you might find that you only have a handful of major problems, and in this case it is obvious what to work on. Instead you might see a multitude of minor problems, in which case it could be a problem knowing where to start. By this stage though you should have a pretty good feel for what is important to you, and let that be your guide.

Initially I was so pleased with myself at having found 'all these problems', that I set about fixing them all at once. This was not a good idea and I was quickly overwhelmed. I learnt the hard way that it is better to fully-sort one problem (so it stays sorted) than to half-fix several (so they creep back in over time). So I now try to focus on one thing at a time, or maybe two.

There is also a case for working on Preparation problems first. As we discussed, a preceding 'mental' error can produce a subsequent 'physical' one. So in some ways it makes sense to prioritise issues to do with the 'choice of shot' or 'setup', over those to do with the 'swing'. But of course if you have a major Execution problem, this might require all your attention.

Finally, I would like to point out that golf professionals can help with most things. Many golfers only tend to think of lessons in the context of full swing improvement, and are perhaps wary of getting drawn in to a long-term programme that might require taking a step backwards before reaping some benefit. But this is missing a trick.

For example, I highlighted in earlier chapters that being able to play well from slopes, bad lies and fairway bunkers can have a big impact on your ability to score well. Also, that three-quarter and low-flighted shots are useful tools to have in your armoury.

These are specific areas where golf professionals are trained to help. So if you don't manage to crack these by yourself, it makes sense to perhaps book a lesson. In my experience even half an hour with a professional, on one or two specifics, will be money well spent.

To summarise, it is important to:
- capture information about the weaknesses in your long game
- consider the problems that are in your control (and exclude those that aren't)
- make an effort to understand the underlying reasons
- appreciate the difference between a Preparation and an Execution problem
- prioritise and focus on the problems that matter most

The smart golfer differentiates between 'Preparation' and 'Execution', and focuses on the problems that have the potential to cost the most shots.

SMART GOLFER CHECKLIST – PRIORITISE AND FOCUS

○ Problems are to do with Preparation or Execution
○ Mental tiredness can affect everything
○ Long established bad habits can get in the way
○ Poor Preparation can result in poor Execution
○ Identify location problems (e.g. tees and approach areas)
○ Look for other problems (e.g. weather and certain clubs)
○ Focus on problems that might cost the most strokes
○ Any way-offline shot has the potential to be costly
○ A poor swing, even with a good outcome, does too
○ Unhappiness with a shot suggests a problem
○ Work on Preparation problems as a priority
○ Consider selective help from a professional

AROUND THE GREEN

A good short game makes all the difference. Making a mess of things from close-in can be expensive, whilst getting 'up and down' is a shot gained. Pitching, chipping and greenside bunker play are critical to scoring well.

19. PITCH SHOTS

A smart golfer knows that distance control is the key to a good pitch shot, aims to the correct area of the green, and has the option to play a 'pitch and run'.

A 'pitch' shot is defined as a shot from 50 yards or less, typically played with a wedge. On the backswing, the hands move up towards trouser-pocket level, but usually stop short of the waistline. Some players describe it as 'a half swing', and it is certainly less than a three-quarter one. But it is also more than a 'chip' (which I discuss in the next chapter).

The importance of the pitch shot varies from player to player, and depends on the course being played. Take for example, a round I played recently on a course that is quite long (measuring 6,600 yards from the tees we played).

One of the players was a 'senior' with a handicap of 12. He tends to hit the ball straight, but not so far. In this round he played no fewer than nine shots to the greens from between 20 and 60 yards. In contrast, another player in our group, who is quite long and has a handicap of 7, played none.

If the course had been shorter (say 6,000 yards), I expect these players would both have played the same number of pitch shots, say four or five. The senior would play fewer because he would have been able to reach more of the greens with full shots. And the long player would have played more, because he would have been closer to some of the greens on par 5s and short par 4s.

So before reading on, it is perhaps worth considering how important the pitch shot is to your own game. For example, is it material to you on your home course?

When required, the pitch shot is important because if it is played well it virtually guarantees that the golfer will get down in three shots, occasionally two. On the other hand if it is misjudged, the player is likely to be in a situation where a difficult 'up and down' remains, or the ball will be on the green but so far away from the hole that a three-putt beckons. The difference between a good pitch and a bad pitch, is a shot lost, or more.

For example let's consider a pitch of 40 yards and assume that a good swing made good contact with the ball (so it got airborne nicely and the shot wasn't 'a duff'). With this type of shot, the majority of golfers are far more accurate with line, than with distance. Even a below-average golfer is likely to have reasonably good 'left to right' accuracy (with the ball heading towards the flag).

But only a minority of golfers have anywhere near the same level of accuracy when it comes to distance. In other words, the ball is likely to stop way short, or go far past. So distance control is a major problem with pitch shots.

A golfer's thinking is often attuned to judging an accurate shot as being one that merely went straight. This is understandable since the vast majority of all golf shots are with a full swing, where the judgment tends to be firstly, *did I make good contact* and secondly, *did it go towards the pin*. With both of these conditions being met, the ball is likely to not be far away from the target since a full swing with a given club will fly the expected distance more often than not.

But the same is not true with a pitch or three-quarter shot. The distance that the ball flies with a partial swing is proportional to how far the club went back, the amount of power applied in the downswing (these factors are both fairly constant in a normal full swing) and the quality of contact made. There is therefore more of a 'skill/judgment' element in pitch and three-quarter shots.

One way of gaining consistency with partial shots is to use a method similar to the one I outlined in Chapter 6 – Shot Variation. This approach advocates developing a repeatable partial swing, using a consistent length backswing. Variations are applied on top of this by using different clubs, gripping down, and taking a slightly longer or shorter backswing.

Irrespective of whether you use this approach or not, 'feel and judgment' have a major part to play in partial shots. So let's consider the pitch shot from this perspective. Assuming a reasonable pitch swing technique, there are two elements to playing a pitch the correct distance. Firstly you have to know, or have a pretty good feel for, the distance you want the ball to fly and the extent you expect it to roll. Secondly you have to match this to a shot you know you can play.

Taking the first element, many golfers just glance at the flag, rehearse a swing, and fire away. A big problem with this is assessing the distance properly. Particularly when there are slopes involved (and there often are), 30 yards can easily look like 40, and vice versa. Playing this way the golfer isn't able to say if his distance problem was caused by not judging the distance correctly, or by judging the distance well and failing to play a shot of the required length.

In some cases both might be wrong, yet things could still turn out well (despite the multiple errors of judgment). For example, if the landing spot was further away than thought, but the shot was over-hit, the two effects could cancel each other out. But at the other end of the spectrum, both elements could work against each other. If the landing spot turned out to be further away than thought, and the shot was under-hit, our golfer will come up woefully short.

So good distance control is dependent on both judging the distance correctly, and being able to pitch the ball this far 'on demand'. This challenge is perhaps one of the most difficult in golf, but here are some thoughts that might help.

To get a better feel for the distance required, and to examine the possible landing areas, the smart golfer normally walks halfway to the green to take a look. This is only 25 yards at most, and doesn't take much time.

From the halfway point he decides on a landing spot, preferably one with as little slope as possible. It could be on the green, or just short of it, depending on the conditions. Before he walks back he makes sure he looks forward to the green, and back to the ball, to capture the best possible 'image' from the middle.

Ideally, a golfer should work out how far the ball needs to fly in yards, perhaps by using a GPS, or by pacing it out. Knowing the distance is helpful to be able to learn and repeat a shot of a similar length next time around.

After returning to the ball, and before playing, the smart golfer fixes his mind on:
-   the picture he has of the shot
-   the distance (i.e. the number of yards)
-   the landing spot

By fixing these three things in his mind, he is able to 'take something' from the shot, whatever the outcome.

If the ball lands on or near the targeted landing area, and finishes near the hole, it is time to register a 'job well done'. In order to re-enforce the positive achievement, and to help him to be able to 'call up the shot' again in the future, the smart golfer might once again recall the distance (in yards) and mentally associate this with what the shot and swing looked and felt like.

In the case where the shot doesn't work out, the smart golfer still learns from the experience. If the ball flew too long or short of the landing spot, next time around our golfer knows to make a less or more powerful swing (or to use a more or less lofted club instead). Similarly, if the ball hit the landing spot but failed to roll enough, or rolled too far, he notes the need to judge the 'roll element' better next time (assuming there wasn't a 'funny' bounce).

This kind of approach to pitching set-distances can be helped greatly by practising. One smart golfer I know practises pitching at a local driving range. He positions himself at the far end bay, well away from other players, and places spare ball-buckets at 20, 30, 40 and 50 yards away from the mat. He practises pitching to these targets, and to the centre of the gaps in between. It is no surprise that this is a really strong element in his game.

If you can somehow practise shots of this length in a similar way, you should soon get skilled at:
- seeing what 20, 30, 40 and 50 yards look like (at least on flat ground), and
- feeling what is required to hit the ball these distances in the air

Ideally you should practise with different clubs, to vary the height of flight. If you can improve to the point where you can get fairly close to each bucket with a range of clubs (between say an 8 iron and a sand wedge), you will have a level of skill that could be a massive boost to your ability to score well within pitching range. The principle of knowing how far you need to hit the ball, and then being able to do so, is sound.

Another important element in the pitch shot is aim. In Chapter 8 – Aim and Alignment, I explained that there are several elements to doing this well.

The first issue to be considered is where we want the ball to finish. The simple answer to this is, of course, as close as possible to the pin. Firstly, it is a good idea to plan for the next shot (hopefully a putt) to be as straightforward as possible. But it also makes sense to allow for an average spread of accuracy with a less than perfect shot.

If the flag is in the centre of a flat green, the obvious thing is to try to land the ball a few yards short of this, and run it up to the hole (assuming there is some bounce and roll in the putting surface). But if the flag is near one edge, and there is trouble on that side, or if there are severe slopes on the green, more thought is required.

The two principles to consider when adjusting aim away from a flag are firstly to avoid trouble, particularly on the 'short-side' (the short-side of the pin is the one that is closest to the edge of the green, particularly if there is a major hazard close to it) and secondly to avoid a tricky downhill putt (downhill putts are usually more difficult than flat or uphill ones).

In other words we should aim slightly to 'the long side of the green' and look to leave ourselves a flat or uphill putt.

The next concern is where to land the ball. The most important factor here is to find somewhere that has a predictable bounce. The green is the most uniform surface on the course, so hopefully you can land the ball here, with enough space to bring the ball to halt without running through to the back.

If there are a choice of landing spots on the green, for example because the shot could be played with a more or less lofted club, then choose the flattest area you can. Landing the ball on a slope risks the possibility of a more variable bounce, which could cause the ball to check up or bounce on more than intended.

If there isn't enough room to land the ball on the green without running way past the flag, a 'pitch and run' might be possible. This is where you drop the ball short of the green and run it onto the surface. A pitch and run shot works well if the ground immediately before the green is hard and has a predictable bounce, for example in the summer.

Whilst this shot is straightforward, many golfers don't execute it well. Firstly this is because it is typically played with a straighter faced club, such as a 7 or 8 iron, in order to provide the forward momentum to take the ball forward onto the green. And many golfers don't practise pitching, let alone with a lower lofted club.

Secondly, this kind of shot is usually not required on inland courses for the majority of the year, when the ground and greens are soft. But when summer starts, and the greens harden-up, normal pitch shots start running through to the back. Around this period it is not unusual to see an average golfer trying a pitch and run for the first time since the previous year, and making a complete hash of it.

In order to get the ball running well when it hits the ground, a subtle adjustment to setup and swing can help. In the setup, try to address the ball more back in your stance, making sure that the clubface still faces the target (note this can require a modest anti-clockwise rotation of the shaft). The changed ball position means that the hands start well in front of the club-head and ball, and try to maintain this position through impact.

These adjustments will help to ensure that the ball gets a good roll forwards, minimising the chance that it might 'check up' and lose momentum on its first impact with the ground. If you can master this shot, you will find that a pitch and run is a valuable tool to have on all courses in the height of summer, and on good links courses all the year around.

The smart golfer knows that distance control is the key to a good pitch shot, aims to the correct area of the green, and has the option to play a 'pitch and run'.

SMART GOLFER CHECKLIST – PITCH SHOTS

O   Walk halfway to get a better perspective
O   Ideally, estimate or know the number of yards
O   Aim to the 'long side'
O   Try to leave the ball below the hole
O   Where possible avoid landing on slopes on the green
O   Understand if a problem was 'execution' or 'judgment'
O   Consider a 'pitch and run' with hard/predictable ground
O   Pitch to 20, 30 and 40-yard targets
O   Practise 'pitch and runs' before the summer starts

20.   CHIP SHOTS

A smart golfer knows the importance of the chip shot, maintains this as a core skill, understands the effect of bounce, and always uses the same type of ball.

Every chip shot is a great opportunity. The better the chip, the better the chance of an 'up and down' with a one-putt. A chip shot is typically played from 25 yards or less, usually directly onto the green. Nearly all rounds have four or five chip shots in them, and some will have twice this number. Next to holing putts, chipping is possibly the best opportunity that a golfer has to reduce his score.

Firstly let's consider the simple greenside chip. I define this as the sort of shot you would hit from the fringe (where there is no particular difficulty with the lie and the ball is only a few yards from the putting surface). This type of shot differs from a pitch in that there tends to be little or no 'wrist break' during the swing (it is played with straight-ish arms – the power mainly comes from rocking the shoulders).

There is a key principle with chipping that many average golfers don't appreciate. Provided the ball is close to the green and lying well, the best approach is to take the least lofted club possible and land a yard or two onto the green, thus maximising the roll of the ball, and minimising its flight in the air.

It has been proven many times that golfers hitting straightforward chips on average get much better results using, for example, an 8 iron, compared to a sand wedge. The reason for the increase in accuracy is down to the ball's 'bounce'. From a good lie, bounce is the most unpredictable element of a simple chip shot. It can easily cause the ball to go long, short or to the left or right. The lower the ball flight, the less the bounce of the ball, and the more accurate you should be.

You may notice that for chips to flat greens, lower handicap golfers routinely maximise roll and minimise flight. For undulating greens they may modify this choice in order to land the ball on a flat area, away from severe slopes in any direction, since a slope is also a potential source of inconsistent bounce. In contrast, higher scoring golfers often persist in using the same wedge for everything, and often don't modify their landing areas to account for slopes at all.

If you don't already follow the low flying approach, please give it a go. On a flat practice green, compare how close balls get to the hole with higher and lower flighted shots, using more or less lofted clubs. Then, find a couple of places to play similar length shots with the same club, one with a sloping landing spot, and the other without, noting (hopefully) that the latter gives a smaller dispersion. Once these principles are understood they tend to become a core part of a golfer's short game approach.

Incidentally, many golfers grip their clubs the same distance up the shaft for chip shots as they do for normal full-length shots. The smart golfer knows that this is missing a trick. Gripping down enables far more 'control' with a chip because the golfer is able to better 'feel' the club-head, and manipulate it more easily using the 'fine muscles'.

So for greater consistency, try the approach of gripping down to say 1/2 inch above the base of the grip. And if you make this change, try to grip down the same amount for each club, so that you get the same amount of increased feel throughout.

Sometimes there is a need to chip the ball so that it lands in the fringe (even though this goes against the principle of landing one or two paces on as discussed above). This most often occurs when the hole is cut near the edge of the green as it faces you, particularly if there is more ground between you and the edge of the green than there is between the edge of the green and the pin itself.

In this case the challenge is to find the best spot to land the ball, ideally at the place with the most predictable bounce. In order to keep the ball running well across the fringe grass, the standard chipping approach can be modified to produce a 'chip and run', much in the same way that we discussed a 'pitch and run' in the last chapter.

In fact the principle is very much the same. Just set the ball back in your stance, make sure that the clubface remains square to the target, and make a chip swing whilst keeping the hands in front of the club-head through impact.

Whilst the majority of chips might be from good lies 'close in' to the green's surface, many will be from awkward positions. The situations are many and varied, and it isn't possible to discuss them all here. But being able to play a chip shot from heavy grass is a skill that all golfers will need on occasion.

Let's say the ball is sitting down and the height of the grass around it is more than the height of a ball. The main problem here is that the arc of the swing (which normally comes in low to the ball) will catch quite a bit of grass before reaching the ball. In the worst case it will slow the club and the chip will be 'fluffed'.

To overcome this, a steeper approach into the ball is required. Since this book isn't about 'technique' I won't give a full explanation here. But it helps to set the ball further back in your stance than normal, probably outside of the back foot, and to 'chop down' into the back of the ball from a steep angle, taking more loft than usual.

The main objective is to make the cleanest possible contact with the ball. It is important to make sure that the club-head keeps accelerating and moving through the impact zone. With this type of shot, it also helps to lower your expectation on accuracy. Even good technique will sometimes not produce a great result from this situation.

I specifically mention chip shots from longer grass because I repeatedly see average golfers struggling with them. This is no surprise since very few of them ever practise chipping from anything other than an ideal lie. And yet they complain when they can't get a shot like this to work on the course.

So next time you practise chipping, make the effort to play shots from the variety of lies that you come across on the course.

Also, at certain times of year the grass conditions change, so do take this into account. For example at several courses in my area the grass can rapidly thicken-up in late spring. In contrast there comes a point in early winter where the grass 'softens' and balls sit more on the soil surface underneath. These changes can catch out even the most experienced of golfers.

Now is also a good time to discuss slopes. If your ball is on an upslope, downslope or sideslope, the same principles apply as were discussed in the Chapter 3 – Slopes. The most relevant of these is to *match the slope* with your stance.

I regularly see golfers on a steep upslope around the green standing vertically upright at address. From this position they often make a complete mess of the shot. With their bodies at this angle, it is easy to hit the ground behind the ball, making little or no contact with the ball itself.

If instead you can match the slope, tilting your spine away from the direction of play, this problem is reduced or goes away altogether. Clearly there is a need to 'better brace yourself' on your trailing leg (this may require some additional flexing of the legs and a repositioning of the front foot). But these adjustments will increase the chance that you get a much better contact.

It is worth mentioning that when you tilt your spine (thereby changing the arc of the swing), the angle that the ball comes off the clubface is different from when you stand upright in your normal plane. So if you are on an upslope, and have compensated by 'matching the slope', take a lesser-lofted club to compensate. On a medium upslope, an 8 iron often works better than a pitching wedge. The same principle applies to a downslope, when more loft should be taken.

On a sideslope, with the ball above your feet, the changed angles will cause the ball to come out lower and more to the left (and vice versa with a ball below your feet). A simple way of compensating for this is to open-up the clubface a bit for a ball above your feet (and close the clubface with a ball below your feet). In order to get a feel for this there is no substitute for placing a few balls on each combination of slope, and seeing how the resultant ball flights vary compared to normal.

Many golfers play with a variety of golf ball types. But with a chip shot, the type of ball you play can make a massive difference. A chip shot with a ball with a hard cover and hard core might come off the clubface a lot faster than one with a soft cover. With different balls the same chip swing can therefore produce different amounts of flight in the air, and roll on the ground. And from close-in, a foot here and there can make all the difference between holing the putt or not.

In the case of a high pitch or a lob shot (which I discuss in the next chapter), you might also be able to see noticeable differences between different types of ball. Those with softer covers will tend to 'grab' the clubface more, resulting in a lower flight. Height is critical to not only judging exactly where a ball will land, but also in being able to clear a possible bank between the ball and the green. Therefore, having a predictable ball flight is important.

I suggest that golfers decide on the ball that suits their all round game, and then stick to this. Some golfers might gain more by having a 'distance ball', either because they hit their long shots straighter or get more distance, whereas others might be better off having more 'feel' from a soft ball around the green. Either way it makes sense to choose the ball that most helps you to minimise your score.

But whatever you do, it is important to give your short game a chance by having the same expectation of how the ball will come off the clubface each time. Switching ball types from round to round, or from hole to hole, is a recipe for inconsistency. This principle also extends to practice. If at all possible, try to use the same make and type of ball for practice as you do in rounds.

Good chipping can really smarten up your scores. One player I regularly play with spends three times as much time practising 'getting up and down' from the edge of the green as he does on all the other aspects of his game. And it shows in his scores.

He may not hit the green as often as some (he has a low approach shot which often runs through to the back or off to the side of the green), but he more than makes up for this with his chipping and close-range putting. If you want to score well, get your chipping in shape, and keep it there.

The smart golfer knows the importance of the chip shot, maintains this as a core skill, understands the effect of bounce, and always uses the same type of ball.

SMART GOLFER CHECKLIST – CHIP SHOTS

- Land routine chips a yard or two onto the green
- Take the lowest loft possible
- Try to avoid landing on pronounced slopes
- Grip down for more control
- From long grass chop down on the ball
- Keep the club accelerating through
- Match the slope and allow for changed ball flight
- Practise chips from a variety of lies and slopes
- Use the same make and type of ball for practice and play

21. LOB AND BUNKER SHOTS

A smart golfer is competent from greenside bunkers, makes sound choices from short-sided positions, and has a lob shot.

Many courses these days are built with raised greens, in the 'American' style. With this type of design the greens' surfaces can be as much as 10 or 20 feet above head height. If you are off the edge of a green like this, and the ball has come all the way down the slope (to what is usually a relatively flat surface at the bottom), then a problem arises.

From this position a conventional chip or pitch typically won't get the ball to fly high enough to clear the bank and get onto the green, a highly lofted shot is required. This is where the 'lob' comes in.

A lob shot differs from a chip or short pitch shot in that it is usually played using a 'lob wedge' (a club with more loft than a sand wedge). The shot requires a longer swing combined with an accelerated 'release' through the ball. As a consequence the ball comes off the clubface at an angle far higher than normal (note you can still attempt to play a lob shot without a lob wedge, but the chances of success are greatly reduced).

If you have a moment I suggest you search on the web for Phil Mickelson and 'flop' (the American term for a lob), to see what the world's best can do with this kind of shot. He is proof that, with the right club, and great technique and skill, it is possible to get the ball to lift off almost vertically.

But the challenge for us mere mortals is simply to get a more-lofted shot than would be possible with our pitch or chip swings.

I learnt the lob shot one day when I was fooling around on the range with a much better golfer than myself. He was stroking a sequence of balls up into the sky at an angle that seemed like magic. He showed me the basics and I gave it a go. Initially I 'bladed' the ball a lot, but after a while I got the hang of it.

I use this shot a lot on courses with raised greens, and more widely from situations where my ball has rolled down the side of a green into a dip. It also helps me to get close to a pin on a regular green if the flag is close to the side I am playing from, particularly if there is a hazard, such as a bunker, in between.

One of the keys to being able to play a lob shot is making sure that you have a wedge that has very little 'bounce'. This is quite a technical term but essentially it means that on a flat surface the front 'blade' of the club is able to easily slide under the ball (without interference from the rest of the underside of the club).

Lob wedges are specifically designed with this characteristic, but sand wedges are built the opposite way, as I will discuss shortly. If you don't follow this explanation, ask someone in a pro shop to explain. It is much easier to understand if you can 'see it'.

Many golfers think that lob shots are 'difficult', and just for better players. But as with many aspects of the short game, provided you learn and practise, away from the heat of battle (for example in the safe surrounds of a driving range or practice ground), it is fairly straightforward with the right club. If you can master the lob shot you will find that it is a formidable weapon.

Both chip and lob shots are made more difficult if they have to be played from the 'short-side' i.e. the side where the pin is closest to the edge of the green. In this situation there is 'not much room to play with'. If the chip or lob shot lands too short, it may get stuck in the long grass or fringe, leaving a further, potentially difficult, 'up and down' challenge. By following the usual approach, many golfers fall foul of this. They aim at a spot near to where the fringe meets the green.

But this shot has little margin for error. With lob shots and delicate chip shots it is not unusual for the ball to come up some way short. The smart golfer realises this risk, and often changes his proposed landing spot from the edge of the green to be much closer to the hole itself. If he plays the shot well, on average he will be faced with a longer putt, having rolled possibly well past the hole. But he remains content because he knows that in the worst case it will only take three shots overall.

If our golfer takes the risky option, this increases his chances of getting up and down first time. But it also brings into play the possibility of taking four shots, and a potential disaster. Clearly there is a balance to be had here, and each individual situation should be judged on its merits. But if it is not unusual to find yourself taking four shots from a short-sided position, it is probably time to re-evaluate your strategy.

This principle also applies to escaping from greenside bunkers. With a flag close-in to the bunker, it is better to risk the possibility of the ball finishing well past the hole, than to fail to get out in the first place. Which brings us to sand shots.

Most mid to low handicap golfers have a perfectly adequate greenside bunker game, it is usually a requirement to get to that standard. But many higher handicap players often fail to get out with their first shots, and sometimes not even with their second. Every failed exit from a greenside bunker is a clear shot lost.

Some courses have many bunkers, whilst others have very few or none at all. Every year I play one or two courses that are completely 'bunker free'. So the extent to which bunkers present a serious challenge will depend upon where you play most of your golf.

There are a variety of shots required from greenside bunkers, depending on the lie of the ball and the height and distance needed to get to the flag. For the vast majority of situations a conventional 'splash shot' will do the trick. Provided you know the right technique, this is a really straightforward shot to play. Despite this, many golfers still struggle with it.

The key thing to appreciate with this shot is that the club only makes contact with the sand, not the ball. The ball merely 'comes along for the ride'. The sand splashes up into the air, taking the ball with it as the club slices through. Hence the term 'splash shot'.

The best way of fixing a problem with sand play, or learning in the first place, is to spend some time with an experienced player, or golf professional. This is simply one of those areas where it is best to let an expert explain things in person. It helps greatly to have someone demonstrate how to play these shots, and to observe and help correct your attempts to get it right.

But the good news is that once a golfer appreciates what's required for this shot, he is likely to retain the skill with little maintenance.

I regularly check my greenside bunker swing is still OK, not least because I need to play bunker shots on most rounds, and I want to do a little more than just get out every time. Apart from checking where the ball ends up, my priority is to look at the strip of sand that has been removed. This is something I learned from a professional quite some time ago, and the process works very well.

I look to see if the missing strip is: parallel to my setup (body) line; about the width of a club-head; ½ – 1 inch deep; about 6 inches long; starts 2 inches behind; and finishes about 4 inches in front of where the ball was. If all these conditions are true, then without fail the ball will have come out quite well. Other than this it is just a question of getting the right height and length (which generally depends on how open I set the clubface at address and the length of my swing).

I also make a point of looking at my 'slices' after bunker shots during a round. This is a great feedback mechanism. It either helps me feel good about the shot, or gives me an early warning if my technique is dropping off. I might even take a second swing in the bunker, striking the sand and trying to take a better slice (the rules permit golfers to do this after a shot provided the ball is not still in the hazard).

Before we leave splash shots, I should mention that it is important to have the right tool for this job. The key thing about a sand wedge is to have good 'bounce' on the underside of the club. Once again this is a technical subject that is easier to understand if you can 'see it', so perhaps ask for an explanation in a golf shop.

In fact the lob wedge and the sand wedge have opposite characteristics on the bottom of the club. To put it another way, a lob wedge is unsuited to a splash shot from a bunker with fluffy sand, and a sand wedge is unsuited to a lob shot from a bare lie. If you get the chance, check this out in practice and see for yourself.

Although most golfers imagine that all sand wedges are the same, they are not. Some are better suited to heavy sand, whereas others work best in light sand. So if you are considering a new purchase, try to match the club up to the conditions you most frequently face in bunkers.

Whatever sand wedge you have, from time to time you might be faced with a course where the sand is different to what you normally experience. A couple of years ago I played at a nearby course where they had recently replaced the sand in half of the bunkers. The sand they used was heavier than the rest and newly laid sand has a tendency to be 'fluffier' than long standing sand. These factors combine to make it extra difficult to slide the club through.

With hindsight it is no surprise that I, and others in my group, failed to get out of several of these new bunkers, despite us all being reasonably good sand players. So if you are playing away from your home course, do take a look at the sand in bunkers before you start. If you think it is heavier or fluffier than your normal conditions, more power will be needed in the swing, and vice versa.

It is also worth noting several other situations in bunkers that might cause difficulty. The first of these is 'compacted sand' which crops up when there isn't a lot of sand in the bunker, or when it has been compressed or compacted (for example from continual use or after a period of heavy rain). Several of the courses I play have good sand all through the season, but in winter it is not unusual for the bunkers to suffer.

So at the end of autumn I try to remember to dust off my compacted lie shot. I either try to 'pick the ball off the surface', or take a lob wedge and make a swing similar to a lob shot (making sure I contact the surface as close as possible to the ball). With a conventional sand shot, the club won't penetrate the sand, and the bounce of the club will most likely result in 'thinning' or 'blading' the shot.

Other difficult situations in bunkers include:
- a ball that is partly or wholly buried in the sand
- a 'fried egg lie' (where the sand looks like the white of the egg to the ball's yoke)
- a ball lodged up in the face of a bunker

Regarding these shots, and maybe with the 'compacted lie' too, it is perhaps best to develop good technique with help. Any explanations I could give here would be inadequate, and not cover all eventualities. This is another instance where it is better to see things demonstrated, and to develop and refine your skills with someone there to point out how issues can be resolved.

Fortunately, golf professionals are well used to giving lessons on this subject. So rather than struggling with lob or bunker shots, it makes sense to perhaps book a lesson.

The smart golfer is competent from greenside bunkers, makes sound choices from short-sided positions, and has a lob shot.

SMART GOLFER CHECKLIST – LOB AND BUNKER SHOTS

O   Develop a lob shot – it is a great weapon to have
O   Have a lob wedge for lob shots
O   Consider playing safe from the short-side
O   Getting out of bunkers first time is the highest priority
O   Learn the 'splash shot', and maintain this
O   Examine 'slices' from the sand
O   Have a sand wedge with the right amount of bounce
O   Examine the sand at unfamiliar courses before play
O   Develop/improve bunker skills with help as required

22.   SHORT GAME IMPROVEMENT

A smart golfer identifies the weaknesses in his short game, and does something about it.

Most golfers would say that they would like to improve their short game, but would they be motivated to do so? This would depend on how much work was involved, what the likely gain would be, and to some extent what time they have to spend on it. In other words, is it worth the effort in the first place?

Hopefully the last few chapters demonstrate that for the vast majority of players the answer is most probably yes. Even taking a golfer with limited time, it is perhaps worth playing only 9 holes instead of 18, and using the time saved to sharpen up on your short game. In order to clarify what you have to gain, it is probably worth considering your current play 'Around the Green'.

The normal way of assessing a player's short game is to understand their 'Up and Down' (U&D) percentage, much in the same way that tour professionals do. For a given round or tournament this figure is calculated by considering the number of shots within 40 yards of the green, and dividing this into the number of times the player gets down in two shots. So if a professional makes six attempts in one round and is successful with two of them, the answer would be 33%.

But, for most golfers, this is a flawed approach. For a start, any player who struggles to break 90 may be more concerned with getting down in three shots, let alone two. Secondly, this measure includes putting, and for now at least we are trying to focus only on short shots.

The U&D ratio also doesn't account for any degree of difficulty. For example, a simple chip from just off the green counts the same as an attempted flop shot off a bare lie or a 30-yard bunker shot from a downhill slope without a proper stance. An alternative is therefore required.

In an earlier chapter, I introduced the Good, Average or Poor (GAP) method as a way of judging your long shots – Good means 'happy with the shot', Average means 'not Good, but not Poor either' (in other words 'OK'), and Poor means 'not happy with it'.

This approach can also be used to assess short game shots. For example applying the GAP approach to chipping, it should be possible to count up your recent shot attempts and get a feel for how good your game is in this area. You could then do the same for other short game shots, such as from conventional lies in bunkers.

For shot types that you play frequently (say half a dozen times a round), this method works fine, albeit you may need to think back over a couple of rounds. But for infrequent shots (such as from a plugged lie in a bunker), it perhaps makes sense to consider another way.

The approach I took was to test myself at my club's 'short game area'. I appreciate I am fortunate to have this facility since many golf clubs don't have one, noting also that many golfers are not members of clubs in the first place.

But in order to improve, practice is required, so I will assume you have some facility, even if you get the job done by finding a quiet green on a course somewhere when it is not too busy. In fact, one of the characteristics of the smart golfer is that he applies his mind well to any problem that might improve his game. So finding a place (and the time) to practise, when other golfers don't, is perhaps another way of 'getting an edge'.

Firstly I decided on the shots I was interested in. To simplify at this point let's just consider three of these: a standard pitch shot (of 30 yards); a simple chip (of 10 yards); and a conventional greenside bunker shot from an average to good lie. I played 10 of each of these shots from average to good lies, rated each shot, and gave myself an overall grade for each category.

The general rule of thumb I use for simple shots from good lies is that if a ball finishes within 10% of the original shot distance from the flag, it should be considered Good. If it is more than 20% away it should be considered Poor, and the remainder are therefore Average. For example a shot from ten paces away needs to finish within about one pace of the hole for it to be classed as Good.

In each group of ten shots there will be a spread of Good, Average and Poor, but I plump for a single grade overall (which might be an 'in-between ranking' such as Good/Average if I think the shots were better than Average, but not quite good enough to be Good).

The actual scale doesn't matter. The main thing is to register *your opinion* of how good (or not) you are with each category of shot, and to have some rational data to support this.

Once I had my ratings, I considered how important each type of shot was to me. At this time I was getting to the green areas comfortably with my full shots (in terms of distance), and I therefore only occasionally needed a pitch. But I was also missing a lot of greens, so many conventional bunker and chip shots were required. I listed these three shot types and rated them against my ability and their importance. The results were as follows:

SHOT TYPE	MY ABILITY/SKILLS	IMPORTANCE TO MY GAME
Pitch	Average	Low
Chip	Good	High
Bunker	Poor	High

From this exercise I could see that there was room for improvement with both my pitching and bunker play, but that if I didn't have much time I was likely to get a better return from addressing my sand shots.

If you are serious about your short game, I suggest you do something similar. For example you might test yourself, or count up your shots over previous and/or future rounds. Simply reasoning what shots you are and are not comfortable with, and 'guesstimating' how frequently you think they will come up in the future, should also achieve the same result.

A comprehensive assessment table might look something like this:

SHOT TYPE	ABILITY/SKILLS	IMPORTANCE
Simple Pitch		
Pitch and Run		
Simple Chip		
Chip and Run		
Chip from Rough		
Chip from an Upslope		
Chip from other Slopes		
Lob Shot		
Normal Bunker		
Compacted Bunker		
Plugged Lie Bunker		

By completing this blank table in the same way as my example above, this should guide you to the gaps and shortcomings in your game. But there are a few points that I would like to clarify before we go on.

Firstly, it isn't necessary to be overly precise with the assessment of shot outcomes. I mentioned the <10%, 10%-20%, >20% method earlier because this gives a good approximation. For example if you are ten paces away and get the shot within one pace of the hole it seems reasonable to say that was Good. But just having a rough sense of Good, Average or Poor is perfectly adequate for most golfers.

This is not least the case because some shots are by their nature more difficult than others anyway. The three shots I used in my example table are perhaps the easiest of all those shown in the blank table. Frankly, if I get a bunker shot from a plugged lie anywhere on the green, let alone near the hole, I am delighted!

Secondly if you are 'testing yourself', pay more attention and give more weight to your initial shots in a sequence. Your accuracy might improve as you get into the swing of things (though if this is a really bad type of shot for you, it equally may not). So if you improve after the initial few shots, you may wish to mark yourself down a bit overall. Your first few shots are more likely to be more representative of what will happen in a round when you haven't played this type of shot for some time.

Thirdly, it is easy to ignore shots that you don't play frequently, particularly if you follow the suggestion of spending time where there is the greatest return. But this could be missing a trick.

There are quite a few shot types that are infrequent. But because there are so many possibilities, there is a good chance that you will encounter one or more of these 'unusual shots' in each round. And since we are talking about short game shots, each time you mess-up it will probably cost you.

Thankfully, the skills required for most of these infrequent shots are, once acquired, retained easily. So after the initial one-time effort to get your skills up to standard, you will hopefully be set for several months or more. You will also have the potential pleasure of (for example) being able to pull a lob shot 'out of the drawer' at a critical time, possibly to the amazement of your playing partners.

Which just leaves the question of ongoing maintenance. It is often said that the short game is the most critical area when it comes to scoring well, and that the majority of time should be spent on this if you are serious about your golf. If you include putting in the definition of 'short game', then I agree with this statement.

The best standard players tend to practise following the time-rule of '1/3, 1/3, 1/3' for 'Long Shots, Short Shots, and Putting'. *If you follow this approach, you won't go far wrong.*

When practising short shots there are a few principles that it is worth bearing in mind. Perhaps the most important of these is to always pick out a landing spot for each practice shot. For each practice shot a golfer should:
- decide on the ultimate target (usually the flag)
- pick out a specific landing spot
- rehearse and 'feel' the shot
- setup up well
- execute and
- assess the shot and outcome

The judgement of whether the shot was executed well (or not) should be mainly based on how close the shot went to the chosen landing spot. If you hit the spot but the ball doesn't get to the flag, this is nearly always an error in reading the shot in the first place (though sometimes an unexpected bounce can take a shot left, right, short or long).

The principle of having an exact landing spot also applies on the course. This way the golfer is able to understand more clearly if a problem was an issue relating to Preparation (including judgment of roll after landing), or Execution.

Secondly, whilst practising try to make each shot 'important'. The reason for this is that each shot on the course is important, so the more realistic you can make your practice sessions, the easier it will be to repeat this in anger on the course. One way of doing this is to practise your short game (and putting for that matter), with a friend. Challenge each other to get closest to the pin, or to get down in the least number of shots.

Thirdly, make practice varied. Practice time is an opportunity to try out different things. Use different clubs to the same target. Play from slopes as well as flat ground. Vary distance and ball flight height with the same club from the same location. Play from typical and poor lies (where poor includes a range of possibilities including long grass and bare ground). Variations like these help to develop the 'fine' skills that are so important with the short game.

Finally, it isn't necessary to practise all the different types of shot on each occasion (though perhaps playing a couple of each of the main types of shot is a good idea if you have time). One way of splitting your time is to pick a few areas (perhaps those you most have a problem with) and get these up to a good state before you move on. A key principle here is to make sure that you have practised each type of shot at least once in every two or three month period.

As you practise, it might become clear that some of your short game shots just aren't working. If so it is probably time to seek some help. If you have friends and playing partners who are proficient in these areas (or ideally expert), why not seek their assistance? There is also the option to work with a golf professional to get things sorted out.

With the short game there is unfortunately no substitute for a) having good technique and b) putting the time in. It is important to recognise and accept this. It might seem obvious, but it never ceases to amaze me how many players acknowledge, year on year, that their short games are holding them back.

The smart golfer identifies the weaknesses in his short game, and does something about it.

SMART GOLFER CHECKLIST – SHORT GAME IMPROVEMENT

O   Assess short game weaknesses by shot type
O   Use GAP principles, and Preparation/Execution
O   Work out the importance of different shot types
O   Always have an exact landing spot for short game shots
O   Split practice time 1/3, 1/3, 1/3 (Long, Short, Putting)
O   Make each practice shot 'important'
O   Vary practice shots: clubs, distances, flights, lies and slopes
O   Rotate, so each shot type is practised over a set period
O   Seek help if required

ON THE GREEN

Sometimes getting the ball onto the green only seems like half the battle. A golfer can play exceptionally well from tee to green but still walk off with a poor score if his putting lets him down.

23. THE PUTTING STROKE

A smart golfer knows how important it is to have a good basic putting stroke – it is much easier to get the ball into the hole with sound technique.

It is a relatively easy matter to answer the question, 'how good a golfer are you?' Your recent scores and your handicap provide a good numeric measure that is easily compared to others. But being clear on the standard of your putting is more difficult.

Golfers typically take anywhere between 30 and 42 putts per round, averaging about 36. The number of putts in a given round will vary depending on:
-   the condition and speed of the greens
-   a player's familiarity with the greens
-   a player's skill at reading and executing putts; and
-   the mix of distances of 'first putts' (i.e. the length of the initial putt on a green)

The rounds when golfers take the fewest putts usually occur when a player's 'approach play' is at its worst. Having missed the green, a golfer is left with a short shot from the surrounds. These shots tend to finish closer to the hole than long approach shots and this in turn makes the length of the subsequent (first) putt much shorter. There is therefore a greater opportunity for one-putts, and it is easier to avoid three-putts all together.

A simple way to get a sense of your putting standard is to compare yourself to other golfers with similar handicaps. Or if you keep track of your number of 'putts per round', you might also be able to spot a trend. Alternatively, you could do something similar to the 'Good, Average and Poor' approach I explain in the last two sections.

Another way of getting a handle on putting ability is to do the '50% test'. Find a gently sloping area on a putting green, and place balls around this, evenly spaced in a circle. Start at three feet from the hole and progressively move outwards in one-foot increments. Noting how many putts you hole and miss, you should be able to find a distance where you meet the 50% threshold, i.e. where you hole as many as not.

For a given golfer this number will vary based on the severity of the slope (more slope = less putts holed) and the quality of the putting surface, but at least it provides some objective measure. I tried this with a group of players who play to a good standard, on a fairly smooth green with some slope. We concluded that for us a figure of six feet was 'very good', five feet was 'good', four feet was 'average' and three feet would be 'poor'.

As with all shots, in many ways the most important measure is how you *feel* about it. Most golfers conscious and subconscious combined should give a pretty good sense of whether they want (or need) to improve their putting, or not. And if you want to get better, a good place to start is by considering the putting stroke.

The *stroke is to putting* what the *golf swing is to the rest of your game*. As can be seen in the rest of the book, there is much that can be done to score better without changing your swing, and the same argument applies to putting. But it is also true that a great putting game can only be built on a sound putting stroke. So this deserves attention.

A good golf shot comes from having a good setup and making a good swing. A good putt also comes from setting up well (aim, stance and posture) and making a good swing (though in this case we call it a 'stroke'). It is in the nature of putting that there is no one single way to setup, or to swing the putter. Because of this, there are many potential problems. In fact the permutations are almost unlimited. Not to mention that each one of these might have alternative solutions.

So in order to develop a sound stroke in the first place, or to substantially improve what you have now, it is almost mandatory to seek some help. In-depth knowledge and experience, and the observations of a second person, are required to correctly diagnose issues and to come up with potential solutions. Therefore, a lesson from a teaching professional makes perfect sense.

Despite this, the vast majority of golfers, even those who take swing lessons, won't consider a session on putting. Of course they may be content with their putting as it is now, but it seems to me that many are not and that most would like to improve, at least to some degree.

A professional I know confirmed this is the case in his experience. He says that no fewer than 80% of his putting lessons are with golfers who have handicaps in single figures. He also added that some players have to be virtually dragged onto the putting surface so he can give them help, despite the fact that it is clear to everyone that there are definite gains to be had (and that after a session nearly all acknowledge that they should have done this a long time ago).

I know that many golfers are reluctant to take a lesson because of the expense, and if there is some fundamental constraint on finance, that is fair enough. But a putting lesson need only be for half an hour (most are), and the benefits are so tangible (in terms of being able to score better), that the logic for taking the leap is compelling. Compared to the amount that golfers spend overall, putting lessons are right at the top of the scale in terms of 'value for money'.

Whether you get assistance or not, it helps to have an appreciation of some of the principles of a sound putting stroke. So here are some of the key elements to consider. Firstly there is the setup, or stance. This should be 'comfortable', particularly if you plan to practise putting to any extent.

A golf professional will, as a first step, look over various aspects of the position you have taken up to putt, and for example consider:
- grip (this is often different to that used for the full swing)
- grip pressure (this should be light, but firm enough)
- feet position (width apart and angle to the aim-line)
- body angle to the aim-line (typically square, or a bit open)
- shoulder position (ideally square to the line, but slightly open or closed is also OK)
- balance (being centred is preferred, both front to back and left to right)

- ball position in relation to eye position (directly over the ball has some benefits)
- ball position in relation to the feet (the extent forward or backward in the stance)
- putter face angle (hopefully at 90 degrees to the direction of the putt)
- putter face loft (preferably not overly lofted or de-lofted too much at rest)
- freedom to make the stroke (not 'cramped', enough room 'underneath' or 'around')

Secondly, there is the stroke itself. Aspects that might be looked at here include:
- the takeaway (deliberate or hesitant, brisk or slow, low enough/not 'picked up')
- head position throughout (this should ideally remain still until the ball leaves)
- body motion (preferably 'quiet', a 'slide' of the body or hips is a concern)
- smoothness of stroke (no jerkiness, either vertically or horizontally)
- accelerating through impact (or certainly not decelerating)
- clubface angle at impact (ideally square and at the slight upstroke point in the arc)
- impact position (preferably a consistent strike on the centre of the putter face)
- length of stoke (both back, and through)
- tempo and rhythm (looking for consistency)
- the follow-through (hopefully a good 'release', with no body lifting or twisting)

This is not an exhaustive list, but shows just how complex it can be to diagnose an issue related to putting setup or the basic stroke (and by now it should be doubly clear why getting some expert advice makes sense).

To summarise, a smart golfer appreciates that:
- a sound putting stroke (and setup) is at the heart of a solid putting game
- expert input might be required to solve problems properly (or to develop sound technique in the first place)

After a successful putting lesson, the smart golfer makes a note of the solution(s), together with the underlying issues that caused the problem in the first place. Since most golfers have spent years putting the same way, there is a strong tendency to 'revert back to type' over time. If, or when, a player's stroke drops off again, these notes can be used to help get back on track, or at least to eliminate old problems that have crept back in.

Another factor that can contribute to getting a good strike on the ball (now assuming sound putting technique) is the putter itself. Having the right tool for the job is most important for this type of shot. Many old style putters do not help as much with putting as the more modern ones. A simple solid blade brass putter, of the type that has been around for 50 years or more, might look good in one way, but in most people's hands it won't do much to help your score.

Two of the main factors that contribute to a good putt are: (1) aiming well and (2) getting a good strike on the ball (so it rolls well). To start with, modern putters offer a variety of alignment aids that help get the clubface square to the line of the putt as you setup to the ball.

Also, the majority of putters these days are designed to have a larger area of forgiveness for off-centre putts. The way they do this is quite technical, but if you look at marketing literature it often refers to 'Moment of Inertia' or MOI, which is a basic measure of this. Having a forgiving putter doesn't remove the importance of striking the ball as close as possible to the centre of the face, but it does mean that when you are a bit out with the contact, the effect is minimised.

When selecting a putter it is also worth considering a few other things. The overall length of the putter is important. For most golfers a certain length will feel more comfortable, so if you plan to change do check out different lengths. Please note that I assume the use of a traditional length putter here. I appreciate that for some a belly length putter or broomstick might suit, but to keep things brief I will restrict my observations to the former type only.

Some might choose a relatively short putter, for example 33" long. This can make it easier to swing the arms freely (because there is more room 'underneath'), and make a more precise strike since the eyes are closer to the ball. Alternatively others might choose something longer, for example 36", because they like the feel of being 'upright', or perhaps wish to preserve a bad back.

Other factors that might be considered in putter selection include:
- the overall weight of the club (too light or too heavy won't work well)

- whether it is face balanced or not (this is a technical matter, but it is important because some players putt with more of a rounded arc in their stroke than others)
- putter face loft (this is also technical – most putters have 3 – 4 degrees of loft, but occasionally players find that more or less works better for them)
- grip size (the majority of putter grips are standard sized, but there is an increasing trend towards 'thick grips' – these can help to take a destructive wrist-action out of the stroke)

If you are considering a new putter, try out as many as you can. Most pro shops will lend you a selection as long as you don't take them away from the club. Many will also offer to help by observing your stroke with different putters, pointing out what seems to be best.

When I selected my current putter I tried out about a dozen possibilities, over several days, and homed-in on what worked. The choice I made (which has stood me in good stead) surprised me in some ways, since my first reaction was that a putter of that shape wouldn't suit me at all.

It doesn't make sense to change putters frequently, or to do so simply in the hope of some improvement. If you have something that works well, then stick with it. But if you feel that a change might do you good, it possibly will.

Some golfers find that it helps from time to time to change and putt for a few rounds with another stick. I do this from time to time, digging an old one out from the garage. I often note an immediate improvement, though this tends to drop off after a while. But interestingly, when I switch back to my usual putter, I seem to end up with much greater focus. And I also get a positive lift because in some ways it is like I have been reunited with 'an old friend'.

The smart golfer knows how important it is to have a good basic putting stroke – it is much easier to get the ball into the hole with sound technique.

SMART GOLFER CHECKLIST – THE PUTTING STROKE

O Develop and maintain a sound putting stroke
O Don't hesitate to seek assistance
O Keep a note of past problems and solutions
O Consider replacing an 'old style' putter
O Before buying, try out a range of possibilities
O Sometimes a change of putter is 'as good as a rest'

24. PACE IS EVERYTHING

A smart golfer knows that pace is critical both to hole short putts and to reduce the likelihood of a three-putt.

A good putt comes from making a *good read* (assessing the putting surface between the ball and the hole), *aiming well* (setting up with the putter face square to the desired line), and *executing well* (stroking the ball down the line at the desired pace).

The two most commonly thought-of factors when it comes to reading and executing a putt are 'pace' and 'line'. Many golfers tend to see these elements as equal, but I would contend that *pace is by far the most important.* Let me explain.

If you take a handful of golfers of the same standard and ask them to putt to a spot, about 20 feet away, you might expect a distribution where their balls finish roughly in a circle around the target. But you would be wrong.

The balls would most probably sit in a clear 'oval shape', with the narrow side from left to right as you look down the line. The range of putt-lengths (long to short) is likely to be at least twice the range of putt-widths (left to right). The variation of pace is therefore much greater than the variation of line.

The likelihood of a three-putt being caused by a problem with pace is therefore much greater than it is with line. This might seem surprising, but the reasons are perfectly logical. Let me explain.

In the execution of a putt, the main determinant of 'line' is the angle of the putter face at impact (a secondary factor is the path that the putter head takes, though this contributes less to the overall result). Therefore with line, the golfer has a head start since (presumably) he will set the putter face square to the desired line before the stroke. He will also (presumably) make a reasonable fist of returning it to the same position at impact.

The same cannot be said for 'pace'. The main determinant here is the length of the stroke and the power applied in the strike. The speed that a ball leaves the putter face is entirely dependent on the physical act of stroking the ball by swinging the putter. In other words, for 'pace' there is no 'anchor' to hang onto (unlike for 'line' where the square putter face provides a head start).

Another factor that causes golfers' imprecision with pace is that many putts are just 'read' from behind the ball. This perspective gives a reasonable view of the potential break of the ball from left to right (or vice versa), particularly if the golfer 'squats-down' when surveying the putt. But to get the best feel for distance, and therefore the required pace, it is best to review the putt from side-on, and preferably to walk to the hole and back.

A large proportion of golfers repeatedly leave their putts short, time and time again. It is unclear why this is the case, even the players themselves can't come up with a reason sometimes. But I am sure that not walking to the hole or failing to see the putt from side-on is a contributing factor. I also suspect that those with a poor basic putting stroke might be worried about hitting the ball way past the hole (for some leaving the putt short seems to be the lesser of two evils).

For short and medium length putts it is clearly important for the ball to have enough pace to get to the hole, to give it a chance of going in. *Never-up, Never-in* is a mantra that continues to be used by golfers all over. Even if you go a bit further past the hole than intended, the return putt is made easier by being able to see the line of break on the way back as the ball slows to a halt.

So what is the ideal, or 'perfect' pace, for a putt? On a relatively flat surface, most golf professionals would advocate rolling the ball so that (if it missed) it would come to rest about 12" – 18" past the hole. During the last foot or so of a putt, the ball slows down to the extent that the slightest bump on the surface can knock it materially off line. So by making sure that it drops into the hole before this can happen, one risk is removed.

There is also a logical reason why the suggested pace is only 12" – 18" past the hole, as opposed to further. The slower the ball is rolling when it arrives at the hole, the greater the chance that it will drop-in if it catches the lip. Plus the further past the hole it rolls, the higher the risk of missing the return putt.

Let's not forget 'line', though. Clearly, if the ball is substantially on the wrong line then it won't go into the hole anyway (which is why many golfers give line equal importance). Also, if a putt is way off line this brings into play the possibility of a three-putt in the same way that poor pace does.

In fact, line becomes more important the closer you get to the hole (and that is not to say that line is anything other than generally important at all times anyway). This is because it is perhaps the critical element in determining whether a level putt goes in the hole, since off line has no chance anyway. But it is only on shorter putts where this really matters.

For golfers with average putting ability, once a putt's length gets to beyond about ten feet, the chances of holing it are only about one in ten. So, considering all the factors that go into making a good putt (including, and perhaps critically, reading the putt in the first place), a small improvement in line accuracy has relatively little effect other than for putts that are close-in.

To some readers the figure of one in ten might seem high, but from my observations this is about right for an average player. Try this out and see what you achieve from this distance. Some golfers will find they only manage to hole one of the ten putts whilst others might manage two, three or even four!

To make this a fair test you should use random locations. There should be some slope on at least half the putts. Note also that if you know the line and pace of the putt in advance, you will have an unfair advantage in comparison to a real situation out on the course.

Perhaps for the reasons outlined above, many better standard golfers adopt the mantra, *pace is everything*. And whilst pace clearly isn't *everything*, it is perhaps the most important element to get right if you wish to score well. In my case, just about every time I hit a putt with good pace I am happy with it, even if it is a bit off line.

By putting with good pace I am assured that:
a) I will hole a reasonable number of putts from close-in (because I am giving them a chance at a sensible pace) and
b) I am never too far away for the return putt (and I therefore manage to keep three putts down to a minimum)

There is one more point to make about the execution of perfect pace. The further away you are from the hole, the more the ideal distance for the putt should revert from the position 12" – 18" past, to (stopping at) the hole itself.

Given the level of inaccuracy with 'distance control', the longer the putt the more the objective for pace becomes 'getting as close to the hole as possible' (as opposed to rolling it at a pace that gives the putt a good chance of 'dropping in as it rolls past').

Most golfers make this adjustment subconsciously in any case. But I mention this particularly because the more precise a player can be in defining what he wants from a putt, the more likely he is to achieve it.

Now it is clear what we want from a putt in terms of 'pace', we can turn our attention to reading the putt. Considering pace only for the time being, there are several factors that contribute to this, plus a few things to also watch out for.

Pace in this instance is just another word for speed after impact. The required speed to stroke a putt a set distance is proportional to three things:

- the distance (to reach the hole, or 12" – 18" past)
- the elevation (more speed is required if the putt has to go uphill, less for downhill)
- the speed of the surface (less speed is required if the green is fast, more if it is slow)

If the putt is relatively short, the distance can be easily seen and accounted for. But for longer putts, particularly if there is a slope involved, it pays to at least walk halfway to gauge this clearly. In fact I advocate that golfers walk all the way to the hole for every putt, as I will explain later.

Upslopes and downslopes (excluding sideslopes for the time being) can often be easily seen for shorter putts. But for longer putts it makes sense to step back, walk around, and do a proper assessment of whether the hole is above the ball (an upslope), or vice versa (a downslope).

By looking 'sideways on', a golfer should also be able to more easily spot a change in level en route to the hole, for example where the ball runs down and then back up to the same level it started at (in which case the starting speed should be the same as for a flat putt).

The speed of the surface can be affected by many things. The most obvious of these is the length of the grass. At the course I play most, the grass is cut every second morning for a large part of the year. Putting early in the morning just after it has been mown can provide a completely different experience to putting in late afternoon on the second day.

In addition to the length of grass, a surface can be faster, or slower if it is dry, or moist. Again on this course there are several greens that are in the trees, with a lot of shade. On some days these greens just don't dry out at all, so compared to the average they can be slow. In contrast, several other greens on the same course are right out in the open – these are therefore exposed to the wind, so the surface tends to dry out faster than average.

There are a couple more things to mention about speed. All greens will be slower when there is dew on the ground, or if it rains. Regarding rain, I often see golfers (unfortunately myself included), struggling to get the ball to the hole after a downpour. Despite the fact that most of us know that this slows the ball down, we seem to remain on 'auto pilot', and stroke away at the same pace as before.

Finally, the direction that the grass on a green is growing, or has been mown, can also have an effect. Without getting too detailed on this, if you putt along a light coloured stripe or area of the green, the ball will roll further than if you putt along a darker one.

The light stripe indicates that the grass is 'combed' away from you, for example as a result of mowing. The lightness comes from the reflected sunlight off the blades of grass. If you look at a stripe from one end it will be light and from the other it will be comparatively dark. On the majority of courses at most times of year this isn't a problem, but when the grass is freshly mown, do watch out for this effect. Note also that the same effect is seen when the grass is naturally growing away (or towards) you, also known as the 'grain' of the green.

The smart golfer makes a particular point of assessing the speed of greens, and spotting situations like those above. If you ever hit a reasonable putt but come up woefully short or go much further past than you imagined, do ask yourself why. The factors I describe in this chapter are probably in play somewhere.

The smart golfer knows that pace is critical both to hole short putts and to reduce the likelihood of a three-putt.

SMART GOLFER CHECKLIST – PACE IS EVERYTHING

○ Pace is more important than line for most putts
○ Routinely assess the speed of greens
○ Good pace reduces the risk of a three-putt
○ Good pace increases the chances of holing a short putt
○ Watch the line of the ball after it rolls past the hole
○ 12" – 18" is the ideal pace for most putts
○ Line becomes more critical the shorter the putt
○ Required pace varies with distance, elevation and surface
○ Beware of shady and exposed greens
○ Adjust pace if it rains, and when the surface is wet
○ Look for 'shine' and stripes on greens

25. READ, AIM, PACE AND LINE

A smart golfer has a routine on the green that covers the important aspects involved in reading and executing putts.

The previous two chapters discussed the putting stroke, and the importance of speed, or pace. On the green these elements come together, with others, to create the overall challenge of making a putt.

Let's now consider 'break'. Break is caused by the sideslopes that make the ball veer to the left or right en route to the hole. In some ways there isn't much to be said about this. A putt will either have no break, some break, or a lot of break, and it will be from right to left or left to right. And judging the extent of break is largely a matter of experience.

But examining the putt 'from the low side' is considered to be a 'must'. By common agreement, a slope is best viewed from the side you expect it to break towards (so in effect a golfer is looking up the slope towards the expected track of the ball, i.e. not down from the other side).

The feet can also help with this 'read'. Standing near the line (say a pace or two away, but not on it) a golfer can attempt to sense the extent of the slope through his feet. Is it mild or medium, and in which direction?

Apart from these two checks, and without getting too technical, there is little more to be done when examining a uniform break along the line of the whole putt. But it should be noted that a putt will 'take more break' (that is veer more to one side) as it slows to a halt. So if the break is more (or less) severe near the hole, allow for a bit more (or a bit less) in your aim.

For breaking putts many golfers aim as though they are attempting a straight putt, typically setting up to an imaginary aim-point in the distance. They then hit the putt starting down this line, and let the slopes do the rest. Other golfers instead pick out an aim-spot within a few of feet of the ball, then either setup square to this, or try to roll the ball over it (these two options being slightly different).

Another technique is to work out where the expected 'apex' of the putt is (that is the highest point in its arc), then to setup on a line pointing somewhere above this, once again using judgment to work out how far this needs to be.

Some golfers putt using an alignment-aid marked on the ball. Several ball manufacturers now pre-print these. Alternatively, some players put a line on the circumference of their balls using a marker pen (there are cheap gadgets that assist with getting a straight line in the right place).

Taking this approach, a player stands behind his ball marker and carefully places the ball so that the marked-line aligns with the start of the chosen line for the putt. The golfer then sets up to the line on his ball. He is now assured that he has setup square to the line of his intended putt.

I tried this approach for some time, but now don't use it. I found I took too much time getting the alignment right and sometimes felt that I had to some extent forgotten the 'sense' of the putt by the time I stood back up again. But a good proportion of professionals and better standard golfers use the alignment-aid process, as does one of my regular playing partners. So if you think it might help, do give it a try, particularly if alignment is one of your big issues.

But with all these techniques, pace is still critical. For a putt with break, if the ball sets off down the chosen line at a speed that is slower (or faster) than required, then the ball will break too soon (or too late), and the possibility of holing the putt will have gone. So once again pace is important, since for a breaking putt the amount of break depends on the pace of the putt.

Most good standard golfers have a 'routine' that they go through before they putt. This is important because it makes sure that each putt is given due respect, and all the elements are considered. Some time ago I realised that I didn't have a putting routine myself, but I do now, and it might be helpful to walk through this as an example.

As I approach the green I am already scanning to see where I think the slopes might be. In fact, I may already have a fairly good idea from watching my or others' pitches and chips running-out on the surface. It helps to take particular note of which way the ball falls towards the end of its roll since this provides a good indicator of both slope direction, and severity. Next I:
- walk up to my ball and mark it (to make sure that there is no problem underneath, and that my ball is clean)

- repair my pitch mark, and any others nearby (out of courtesy to all)
- walk to the hole, on the low side of the putt (if there is one)
- look from beyond the hole back to my ball along the line
- on the way back pause at the halfway mark and look, from the side, along the length of the putt to see if the hole is above or below my ball's position (to determine elevation) and to gather information about the possible break

I then return to my ball, and stand behind it, trying to visualise the line of the putt at the speed required to get it to the hole.

This completes the 'read' element of my routine. I then go into 'execution mode'.

Standing behind the ball, with the hole directly beyond it, I rock the putter back and forth in my hands, looking up and down the line of the putt, imagining the roll of the ball. In effect I am trying to 'feel the putt' in advance. You will notice that professionals also do this, not least because by consensus this is perhaps the best way to fix the required pace in your mind.

Some players 'feel' and 'see' the putt standing side-on to the line, but the majority stand with their bodies facing the hole. The latter approach is perhaps better since, according to vision experts, distance and speed are best judged using full binocular vision (in other words with both eyes fully engaged).

Finally, I move in, setup square to the line I have chosen, take a last look at the hole, remind myself that 'pace is everything', and pull the trigger. Note: the reason for my last thought being about pace is that the line should take care of itself (assuming my aim-line is correct and that I have successfully setup square to it).

After the putt I try to assess how well I have done. I say 'try' because this isn't always the highest priority on my mind at this point. Nevertheless I know this helps, so I try to persist with it.

The first thing to consider is, *did I put 'a good roll on it?* In other words, *was it a good putting stroke?* As I explained in Chapter 23 – The Putting Stroke, a good roll is the measure of a good stroke. If nothing else I will hopefully be happy with the outcome of this assessment. If I am repeatedly not satisfied, this suggests that I need to look at my putting technique.

Next I ask myself, *did I read the putt correctly?* In other words, assuming it was a relatively good stroke, did the track of the ball correspond to what I had predicted before the putt. This is important since if I have read the putt incorrectly, I would like to know why (so I can hopefully get it right next time).

After this I consider the pace and line of the actual putt. I ask myself, *did I roll it down the line I selected?* I can usually tell if I pushed or pulled the putt, and this should in any case be shown by the putt setting off to the right or left of my intended line. I also ask myself, *did I stroke the putt the right distance*, in other words, did I put the pace on the ball that I had wished for?

This all sound quite complicated, and I guess in some ways it is. Even though I have been doing this for some time, I still find it is not possible to do all of these steps all of the time. But at a minimum I try to walk onto each green with the four words in this chapter's title clearly in my mind, namely: **Read, Aim, Pace and Line.**

I find that these cover nearly all the aspects of what is required *before and after* a putt. So if I can just remember these words I usually make a reasonable fist of things.

Before each putt I try to make sure that I thoroughly **Read** the putt, so I know where to **Aim**, then setup square, and try to roll the putt down the **Line**, at the right **Pace**. Afterwards I try to evaluate if my **Read, Aim, Pace and Line** were all correct.

This is clearly only one example of a pre and post-putt routine but all approaches tend to cover similar ground. Obviously each golfer should do what suits him best. But if you can in some way incorporate the principles discussed above, you hopefully won't go far wrong.

The smart golfer has a routine on the green that covers the important aspects involved in reading and executing putts.

SMART GOLFER CHECKLIST – READ, AIM, PACE AND LINE

- O   Examine putts 'from the low side'
- O   Use your feet to gauge the slope's extent and direction
- O   Read putts thoroughly, have a routine
- O   Include green speed, distance, elevation and break
- O   Visualising and 'feeling' a putt beforehand can help
- O   Setup with good alignment
- O   Assess putts afterwards: read, aim, roll, pace and line

26.　　SHORT PUTTS

A smart golfer knows that, perhaps more than anything else, holing short putts is the key to a good score.

Failing to hole short putts (say from less than four feet) is one of the most damaging things that can happen in a round – each time a shot is lost. In the same way, holing a slightly longer putt (say up to eight feet) is a shot gained. In scoring terms, putts within this range are a really big deal.

But it is not just about scoring. Every time a short putt is holed, or not missed, a golfer's sense of well-being and confidence rises, or remains intact. More than anything else, these putts can be the making of a round. So there is a great opportunity here. The smart golfer does everything he can to perform well within this range.

With hole-able putts, sound technique is key. Building on the previous three chapters, if a player can make a solid putting stroke, resulting in a good roll, at the right pace, down a reasonable line, then there is every chance of success. But what else do smart golfers do to increase the proportion of putts they hole from this distance?

Firstly, it seems to me that players who putt well from close-in are particularly well focused. The way they read and approach putts is efficient and confident. There is little doubt in their minds that they will, at a minimum, make a good attempt at it.

Their eyes seem to be fixed on the line between ball and hole, and the hole itself. Many form an image of the ball going into the hole. This isn't just a vague notion of a good result, but a clear picture.

One golfer I know selects and then focuses on a spot at the back of the hole, just below grass level. This could be part of a root sticking out, or some discolouration in the soil, the key thing is that it is a small spot. He imagines the ball striking this at perfect pace. For putts with break, he chooses a spot allowing for the ball's final angle of approach. Before pulling the trigger on a really short putt, he zooms in on this spot, and thinks of nothing else.

Some players focus more on the track of the ball. Their eyes go back and forth to the hole, scanning the anticipated line. I read somewhere that doing this at the same pace as you expect the putt to roll helps. As does seeing the ball 'rolling over the lip' and 'pouring' into the hole, again allowing for the final angle if it is a breaking putt.

Other golfers tend to think more about rhythm, perhaps thinking something like, *back (pause), and through,* (spoken in the mind, with the same tempo as for an 'ideal' stroke).

Some will undoubtedly have the odd 'swing thought' too, such as to accelerate through impact (since decelerating almost certainly will produce a poor result), or to concentrate on striking the ball out of the centre of the putter (since this gives an improved chance of a good roll).

But it is also important to not have a cluttered mind. For a long period I was a slave to swing thoughts, and sometimes ended up tying myself in knots.

During one period I so wanted my putting mechanics to be good that, by the time I finally setup for the stroke, I had forgotten the extent of break that I had read into the putt in the first place. Having then re-fixed this in my mind, I sometimes found that I had lost all sense of the pace required. There are no prizes for guessing that this was not one of my best periods on the greens!

These days one of my key thoughts before I pull the trigger on putts from close-in is, *it's line and pace and pace and line.* I find if I say both of these things in my mind, or even under my breath, the combination somehow helps me to get both things about right. It certainly removes the possibility that I get 'line locked' (a problem where a golfer concentrates so much on the line, that he fails to stroke the ball at the right pace).

After setting up square, it makes sense to scan the line of the putt. But note that this should preferably be done by turning the head only. Many average golfers turn their shoulders and body towards the hole during the process, then fail to turn fully back. Their 'nice and square' setup is now somewhat 'open' to the line, which can create a problem.

The same goes for watching the track of the ball after impact. Again it makes sense to just rotate the head (as opposed to turning the body to look). This reduces the possibility that an early glance might affect the swing itself, throwing the putt off line.

Apart from the rocking motion with the shoulders and arms, all good putters tend to remain completely still throughout the stroke. On short putts many don't look up until the ball has gone, and some even wait to hear it drop into the hole. This is an interesting approach in that it shows that the golfer has a clear set of priorities.

There is a conflict between the desire to see the roll of the putt, particularly to a positive conclusion, against giving it the best chance of success (which by implication includes trying to remain as still as possible throughout the putt). I admire players who are able to do this, but I feel that I at least need to get some feedback on roll, line and pace (so that if I miss, I have a better sense of why).

What I tend to do is to say to myself, *look only after the ball leaves.* In order to help with this some golfers make a point of waiting until they get a glimpse of the grass underneath the ball, after it has gone.

Good putters also seem to be calm over short putts. I can tell when some players are about to make a bad putt by observing their breathing. If this gets shallow, that's a sign that stress is getting the upper hand. In fact some golfers stop breathing altogether over a short critical putt. They take a breath in as they settle down, but concentrate so hard that it doesn't come out until after the putt has gone.

Poor breathing tends to create tension that invades the shoulders and arms, making a free flowing stroke more difficult. This can also result in a player gripping the putter so tightly that his first movement inevitably becomes a jerk. Breathing well also helps with keeping a clear mind. So over short putts, it can help to try to relax your grip and retain a steady breathing pattern throughout.

The smart golfer is also doubly clear about what they want to achieve with a putt. This might seem obvious (because we all want our putts to go in all of the time), but sometimes a compromise is needed.

Take for example, a tricky six-footer across a fast slope, perhaps where you are also a bit suspicious of the surface. In one way you want to give the putt a good chance of success, but in another you want to avoid the possibility of a tricky three-foot return.

I frequently see average golfers struggling with these sorts of putts. As a consequence they sometimes end up doing neither thing well. A typical result is where the ball sets off on the line to best hole the putt (in other words with the line that would work with 'a 12" – 18" pace'), but it is only struck 'at dead weight', and thus falls away weakly below the hole.

The same dilemma occurs with flat putts that are in between 'go for it' and 'lag it' range. The golfer wants to have the chance of holing the putt, but at the same time doesn't want to risk a three-putt by running it too far past. This conflict often breeds indecision, which in turn can lead to a bad putt.

So it makes sense to have a clear goal. If you want to hole a putt, give it full weight. If you want to lag a putt, hit it at dead weight. Or compromise, and make your intended pace such that the ball would finish 6" – 9" past the hole. In this way you slightly increase the chances of leaving the ball short (and of the ball veering off line a few inches before the hole), but at the same time reduce the risk of going too far past.

Finally, it pays to try to *give every putt respect*. By that I mean your full attention and focus. This is quite difficult to achieve in practice, noting that there are 36 putts or so in an average round, not to mention all the other things to think about. But I mention this because I have observed there is a clear correlation between making a good putt, and being focused.

For example, I have seen golfers lose focus on the green when:
- it is a very casual round (so there is nothing riding on the hole)
- they are mentally tired (and the mind starts drifting)
- they feel physically tired (and as a consequence don't walk all the way to the hole to read a long putt)
- they have just hit a poor shot (and in their disgust they 'check out' mentally)
- they are last onto the green, but first to putt (and therefore feel rushed)
- there is a lot of 'chat' (and they are distracted or drawn into it)
- the opposition are doing badly (this takes the pressure off and there is a tendency to 'relax')
- the opposition have repeatedly done very well (this can grind a golfer's spirit down)
- they think they can't 'half' the hole (for example because their opponents look certain to go one better)
- faced with a four-footer when their partner, who is a good putter, has a three-footer for the same score (so they think it doesn't really matter)

But if you want to excel at putting, you need to adopt the attitude that *every putt counts,* and that *every putt deserves respect.* Each putt is a chance to test yourself, and to learn.

Smart golfers give even their short putts a high level of respect and, guess what? They tend to make more of them than others who have the same core putting skills. This respect extends to properly reading a putt, even if it's only a couple of feet and you think you know the break or line already. It also means going through your normal routine – I repeatedly see golfers of all standards missing short putts because they haven't done this. And every missed short putt is a shot gone!

There is one more thing that can help with short putts. It helps to have a 'no gimmes' rule in friendly rounds (where every ball has to be holed out, even from a foot or so from the hole). Getting agreement to this from all players can be difficult, but everyone benefits. Generally this will mean that you are all better prepared for proper competition rounds, and for 'not so friendly' matches when you might be suddenly faced with 'having to putt out'.

I play a lot of match play golf. In friendly games it is common amongst regular players to concede short putts of less than three feet. As a consequence putts from this length (and even closer to the hole) can easily become a problem in the heat of competition.

Because these putts tend to be given in friendlies, many golfers don't have the chance to practise them in their regular golf. So these players are not used to confidently stroking short putts when the pressure is on. Practising before play can simulate the physical act, but not the mental challenge in the heat of a round when putts really matter.

In a match, some golfers will know (possibly subconsciously) that this length is usually 'given', and perhaps be standing there wishing that the opposition would give it to them, possibly being vexed because they haven't. Thoughts of possibly missing begin to appear, tension rises and a poor putt can result (I've witnessed and experienced this many times, from both sides of the problem!).

It might require fortitude to get your partners to agree to a 'no gimmes rule', but if you can play this way, everyone will benefit in the end.

*The smart golfer knows that, perhaps more than anything else, holing short putts is **the** key to a good score.*

SMART GOLFER CHECKLIST – SHORT PUTTS

○   Holing short putts makes all the difference
○   Sound technique is the main building block
○   Have some key thoughts, but keep it simple
○   Think *line and pace and pace and line*
○   Have a clear objective, either: 'hole it' or 'lag it'
○   Give every putt respect
○   Setup square to the initial line
○   Rotate the head, don't turn the body
○   Breathe well and relax the shoulders, arms and grip
○   Watch out for 'loss of focus' situations
○   Whenever possible play with 'no gimmes'

27.   PUTTING MATTERS

A smart golfer knows that a positive attitude towards putting, and adequate practice, are both necessary to succeed and properly enjoy the game.

The best putters love putting. But are they good putters because they love putting? Or do they love putting because they putt well?

There was a period when I was 'out of love' with putting. I had just got my long game to quite a good standard. Some days I managed to hit as many greens in regulation as I missed. Partly because of this my expectations rose, and I expected more from myself on the greens too. But no matter how hard I tried; I still seemed to have the same old problems.

After a while I got down on myself. It came to the point where I looked forward to each tee and approach shot, but my shoulders would droop as I approached the green. I remember thinking at one point, *I wish this game was just a test from tee to green – I'd be quite good.*

Then one day I heard someone on the television, a former top golfer I think, saying, *of course if you want to be a great putter you have to love putting.* He went on to point out that any golfer who approached a putt in a negative frame of mind isn't going to do well, no matter how good their technique is. He added that even great putts don't drop into the hole sometimes.

Sad as it was to admit, I had got into a state where I was fearful of missing putts, not just once in a while, but virtually all the time. I was quite a mess. But this person was saying that if my technique was reasonable (and I knew it was), it was just a question of attitude. Once I 'got' this message my problems started melting away. It was like a weight had been lifted from my shoulders.

All of a sudden it was clear to me that I could make a good read, setup well, stroke it down a good line, at good pace, and that sometimes I would inevitably miss. I also started to see that I holed some putts despite not stroking them down the line or at the pace I had intended. My perspective on putting changed from being negative, through to neutral. As I went onto greens I began to be more curious about what would happen, as opposed to being apprehensive.

This was a few years ago now, and I still wouldn't say I wholeheartedly love putting. But these days I walk onto greens with a positive attitude. My manner could perhaps be described as one of hopeful expectation. So I would say that you don't have to love putting, but you certainly can't dislike or fear it.

Even with a good putting stroke, and good confidence, there are times of the year when all golfers struggle on the greens. For me this is most noticeable in the winter months. As we get towards the end of October, grass growth slows down, and the surfaces get bumpy. It is no coincidence that the number of players moaning about their performance on the greens also goes up around this time.

I have tried many times to 'putt my way' though this period by (as I used to see it), rising to the challenge. But from discussing this with other golfers and observing the reality (that putts just go more off line in this period), I have become more sanguine about it. As a result I can regularly be heard saying, *don't beat yourself up about putting during the months between November to March, it just isn't worth it.*

This also extends to there being little point in working on your putting technique over the winter. In order to be sure you're making a better strike, you need to be able to distinguish a good from an average roll, and that is much more difficult when the greens are uneven.

But that doesn't mean there is nothing you can do with your putting in this period. In fact it is a great time to polish up your pre-stroke routine. Instead of being wholly concerned about whether the ball goes into the hole, define 'good' as having been through a comprehensive routine. In doing so you might just improve your percentage holed in any case!

Another period that catches players out is when the greens speed up in late spring or early summer. This is mostly as a result of the greens being cut a few millimetres lower than they are over winter. Around this time it is not uncommon to hear cries of, *you wouldn't believe how fast they were,* and *I three putted so many greens today.*

The smart golfer tries to get ahead of the game here. He will either find out when the greenkeeping staff start cutting the grass to a lower height, or make a particular point of watching out for this. As soon as it happens, he will plan a few practice sessions, spread out over a few days, that needn't be long. It usually takes some time to adjust to the new speed because the judgment of pace goes quite deep in golfers' minds – it isn't just a case of simply remembering to 'give it a bit less'.

Spring is obviously a good time to get your putting technique in shape after the winter. For some this will just be a case of doing what they do at the start of every season, including a practice putting session or two, and spending a bit more time than usual on the practice green before a round. Aside from technique, there are a couple of approaches that I find most helpful in sharpening up.

Firstly, I have a session just concentrating on pace. Initially I make some short and medium length putts on a flat part of the green where I make my judgment of 'good' based on, *did I roll it the right distance?* During the process I try to strike my putts as much as possible out of the centre of the putter face (since this is the most important factor contributing to pace other than the length of the stroke).

For putts nearer the hole, I try to achieve a pace that will take the ball 12" – 18" past (if it doesn't hit the hole). For longer putts, I try to hit the ball at 'dead weight' (or possibly so that it finishes a few inches past the hole). I explained a couple of chapters ago the importance of pace – I know if I can get the measure of speed on a flat surface to begin with, I will from then on be practising from a solid foundation.

To sharpen up my accuracy, I might also try a bit of 'spot putting'. Rather than putting to a hole, I put a small coin or ball marker down (the smaller the better) on an unused area of the green. By placing it away from the hole surrounds I can avoid the worst of any wear and tear.

I then make putts 'around the clock face', from ten feet and in, trying to roll the ball over the marker. If you try this in both flat and sloping areas, you will see just how much more difficult it is to be accurate if there is break involved. Provided this goes well, the spot putting exercise gives me confidence that getting the ball into the hole (that is nearly five inches across) will be an easy matter in comparison.

As discussed previously, given the importance of long and very long putts (in avoiding three putts), it makes sense to also include some from these lengths in any routine. If you find you struggle with these, in comparison with shorter putts, it might be because you need to modify your putting stroke a bit.

Many golfers find that their usual putting stroke works up to a certain length, after which it feels 'different', and perhaps less fluid. In my case I resolve this by setting up with the ball a bit further away from my body. This gives my arms a better chance to swing all the way back and through, without getting caught up in my chest.

Finally, it helps to make your practice as meaningful as possible.

That means testing yourself, and trying to give your best on each and every putt. Even on the practice green I try to make sure that I go through my proper routine for some of my putts (including reading distance, elevation and break). The more I read a putt beforehand, the more I learn.

A good way of sharpening up is to practise together with a friend. Towards the end of the session challenge each other to a putting competition, mix up lengths and slopes. There is nothing like wanting to win, or not lose, to create good focus.

The smart golfer knows that a positive attitude towards putting, and adequate practice, are both necessary to succeed and properly enjoy the game.

SMART GOLFER CHECKLIST – PUTTING MATTERS

- ○ Love putting, or certainly don't fear it
- ○ Great putts sometimes don't go in
- ○ Poor putts sometimes end up in the hole
- ○ Problems are due to read, execution, or both
- ○ Expect to putt less well in November to March
- ○ Use the winter to sharpen up on routine
- ○ React swiftly to faster greens in late spring
- ○ Practise putting, it's important
- ○ Putt from all distances, on a variety of slopes
- ○ Practise for pace only, at least some of the time
- ○ Use a coin or ball marker to sharpen accuracy
- ○ Make practice meaningful

THE BIGGER PICTURE

An experienced golfer is well prepared. He knows the value of 'routine', is aware of his physical and mental state, and adopts a rational and positive attitude. He also shows consideration for others, has integrity and knows the rules.

28. PREPARATION

A smart golfer is well prepared, relaxed, unhurried and ready to play.

Good preparation before a round enables a golfer to free his mind and to concentrate on just playing golf. Shifting mental or physical effort away from the immediate build up to tee-off, helps to minimise stress and maximise the prospect of playing well.

Therefore the smart golfer is organised before he leaves home. He packs his bag early, often the night before. He has gloves, tees, pitch-mark-repairer, marked golf balls, and drinks and snacks, in pre-determined pockets in his golf bag. The grips on his clubs will be in a good state and the studs in his shoes will be well maintained.

He will have looked up the weather in order to understand what he can expect, noting the wind's strength and direction, and the possibility of rain. He has appropriate clothing in order to be warm and dry, or cool and comfortable, depending on the time of year. If he is playing a new course, he will look up the club's website to get a feel for its facilities and rules, and possibly to see some images of the course and its layout.

A smart golfer is unhurried. He is aware that not having enough time pre-round can be frustrating, and might cause him to get off to a poor start. He therefore is clear about his start-time, who he's playing with, and the format of the round. He will have worked out when he needs to set off from work or home to arrive at the course in plenty of time. If he hasn't played for some time, or it is part of his routine, he will also allow sufficient time to warm up before play.

The smart golfer is clear what he wants to get out of the day. He might want to fully challenge himself, and give full attention to absolutely everything he can. Or he might simply want to play and enjoy himself, and thus be more relaxed about making mistakes.

If he is in the process of a swing change, he might decide that his priority that day is merely to try this out on the course, and that everything else is therefore secondary. To help with this he might have a (short) list of 'swing thoughts', either written down or fixed in his mind. He might also allow more time to rehearse the changes before his round starts.

It is an interesting question whether to warm up as a general rule, or not. I have considered and discussed this at length and there is no clear answer. Some players always plan to spend time at the range before they play, and are disappointed if they can't. Others never warm up and it doesn't seem to harm them.

Warming up can be a double-edged sword. If you strike the ball well at the range, you should be in a good frame of mind on the first tee. But if warming up goes badly you have a problem. It is likely that you will start your round with low optimism, and things could spiral down from there.

I have concluded that for most golfers it is best to have a clear policy either to always warm up, or only to do so occasionally. If you often struggle to find the time to spend 20 minutes at the range before a round, it is perhaps best to assume you won't manage it, so don't plan to. But if warming up gets you 'better in the swing of things', and more often than not you can make the time, perhaps build this into your routine.

If you don't warm up, your first shot of the day will be on the first tee. If you usually handle this well, that's fine. If not, it is worth considering if something can be done about this. One golfer I know doesn't warm up as a rule, but is generally excellent with his driver on the first tee. This wasn't always the case, but he came up with a way to overcome the problem.

Like most serious golfers, he practises at a range from time to time. When he does he makes sure that his first shot there is with his driver – simulating the situation on the first tee. Before this swing he goes through his normal process at the first tee. In particular he selects a playing line, tees the ball up, visualises the shot, walks in from behind and takes up his stance with good posture.

Whilst this approach might seem 'over the top', there is no doubt that it prepares him well for days when he doesn't have the chance to warm up. Not surprisingly he is now very good from the first tee, irrespective of the situation.

Whether you warm up at the range or not, taking 10 minutes on the practice green before you walk to the first tee will be time well spent. If it is important to you to score well, it doesn't make sense for your first putt of the day to be on the first green.

Before you putt, it is helpful to get a feel for how chips are likely to behave by seeing what the 'bounce and roll' is like on the practice green. The surfaces can vary considerably from day to day or week to week, for example after heavy rain or when there has been some maintenance. It is easy to drop a shot with an over-hit or under-hit chip early in the round.

Provided the golf club allows chipping on the practice putting green, it is a good idea to chip a few balls from the edge to get a feel for things. If chipping isn't allowed, you can still get a reasonable sense of things by throwing (underarm) a few balls onto the surface. I do this as though I am just getting a few balls out of my bag and onto the green for putting practice – to date no one has objected.

Now it is time for some putts. But how should you spend the time that remains to best effect? To some extent this should be driven by your particular strengths and weaknesses with putting.

To illustrate this point I will relate a conversation I had recently with an 18-handicap golfer who was adamant he could score much better by, *just reducing the number of three putts.*

He explained what he does on the practice green before he starts a round. In common with many other golfers he just putts between the flags, which are normally spaced six or seven paces apart, then 'tidies' the return putts into the hole (these short putts are typically less than three feet away). Yet in our conversation it became apparent that neither of these lengths are a problem for him at all. His main problems are:

- getting the ball to within four feet from a long way away and
- holing out from more than four feet away when he fails to get close enough

Having discussed this it became obvious to both of us that he should change what he does before a round. He should spend the majority of his time:

- putting from one side of the practice green to the other (to sharpen up on the long putts that he struggles with) and
- putting from between four and eight feet (to improve his chances of success from this distance)

In other words he won't spend much time on putts from six or seven paces or on repeatedly (and successfully) holing out from within four feet. This is a complete turnaround from his old approach and illustrates that it is worth thinking about how best to use your (precious) time on the practice green before a round.

If you have no particular issues with your putting, the following is a reasonable routine that should cover most bases. Firstly, get a feel for green speed. This is best done on a flat part of the green taking any slopes out of the equation. Putt a set distance (of say four or five paces) and ask yourself what you think of the green's speed. Is it average, above average, or below average?

Next try a few uphill, downhill and side-hill putts. By the time you have done this you should have a pretty good feel for both speed and break. Afterwards move in to sink a few putts from close range. Whilst doing this, it helps if you can try in some way to make these seem important. In other words, don't just putt away indifferently – apply some focus.

Lastly, before leaving for the first tee, don't forget to roll a few long putts, for example from the far side of the green back towards the fringe near your bag.

The smart golfer is well prepared, relaxed, unhurried and ready to play.

SMART GOLFER CHECKLIST – PREPARATION

- Do everything possible beforehand
- Take appropriate clothing and a well-organised bag
- Have a policy for warming up, or not
- Allow enough time to do everything you want
- Spend at least five minutes on the practice green
- Check bounce and roll on the green (for chipping)
- Understand the speed of the greens
- Concentrate on the things that matter most
- Try some short putts, with purpose
- Roll some long putts, focusing on distance

29.   *ROUTINE*

A smart golfer moves calmly and smoothly around the course, making everything appear routine.

Everything the smart golfer does seems routine. He parks his bag, trolley or golf cart in the most convenient place for the next shot or hole. He is aware whose turn it is next. If help is needed with searching for a ball, he is there. He also offers and is ready to play out of turn if that will speed things up. His whole round seems to be considered, deliberate and efficient.

By thinking ahead our smart golfer has more time to reach better decisions. This approach also helps him to reduce the possibility of coming under personal time pressure. At all times he seems to be calm and unhurried, yet he is always 'up with the pace'. He starts thinking about his shot before reaching the playing area.

By the time he arrives at his ball, the smart golfer will have formed a rough plan by asking himself questions like:

- *What are the options from here with a good or bad lie?*
- *Where is the wind coming from?*
- *Is there a slope, and is it uphill or downhill to the green?*
- *Where are the real trouble spots that I must avoid?*
- *What are the pros and cons of going for the green?*
- *If I need to layup, where is the best or safest place to do this?*

- *Where should I aim so that I finish below the hole, and not be short-sided?*

The smart golfer normally parks his bag or golf cart a set distance away from the ball, on a particular side. He confirms his yardage, goes through his checks, chooses his shot, and pulls his club out (which is perhaps a sign that he has now committed to the shot). He may, or may not, have a rehearsal or practice swing. He then moves in to the ball, typically from directly behind, makes sure he is well-aimed and aligned, takes a last look at the target, and pulls the trigger.

A proportion of golfers make one or two rehearsal swings whilst thinking about the shot. Others wait until they are certain before pulling a club out. Some golfers make full rehearsal swings, whilst others do partial ones (just to get a rough feel for the club or swing). Some do this beside the ball, whilst others do so meticulously from a position directly behind.

When he is ready to move in, our golfer might approach the ball from the side, or from behind, or have no favoured direction. He may or may not have a method for aiming, and (unfortunately) this may or may not be consistent from shot to shot. After moving in, the player might take one last look at the target, or several.

The smart golfer is likely to have a pre-shot routine that brings order to this potential chaos – this helps him to concentrate and handle stress when the pressure is on. Once he has decided what shot to play, he goes through a series of steps that seem to go like clockwork.

There is little doubt that nearly all golfers would benefit from having such a routine. Inexperienced golfers have a golden opportunity here. If you haven't played much golf before, I strongly suggest you develop one.

For more experienced golfers though, the problem is different. If you have played a lot, and don't have a regular routine, then the challenge is arguably much greater. The reason for this is that your current routine is 'no routine', and you will have a tendency to revert to this. So in some way you might need to 'unlearn' what you did in the past.

There are many possibilities for the sequence and content of a routine for playing a shot. Using the Preparation and Execution stages that we have discussed before, the following steps are typical:

Preparation:
- assess ground factors
- work out the effective distance
- consider shot options
- make choice
- get ready/rehearse
- take aim and setup*

Execution:
- take aim and setup*
- have a last look at the target
- swing (takeaway, backswing, downswing, follow-through)
- assess the shot afterwards

....

*Note that 'take aim and setup' could be considered either as part of Preparation, or Execution.

For some golfers it might be helpful to split Preparation into two or more stages. This would allow the player to concentrate on just one aspect, for example either:
-   getting the choice of shot right, or
-   better preparing for the shot itself

In this instance Preparation -> Execution might instead become Shot Choice -> Get Ready -> Swing.

At this point it might be helpful to ask yourself what you do now? Irrespective of the current way you do things, if you think you might benefit by improving your pre-shot routine, you almost certainly will. Just thinking this through in the first place might highlight an obvious improvement.

Some time ago I considered my own routine and quickly realised I was all over the place. Thinking about what I did and didn't do, it became apparent that I was unable to say if I had prepared well for a shot, or not. I therefore couldn't be certain whether or not poor preparation was a factor that contributed to my poor shots.

So I worked out a routine to be more thorough. My objectives were to:
-   minimise the time after I reached the ball (because I don't like being rushed and others don't like slow play)
-   reach sound decisions (or at a minimum to be committed to the shot)
-   rehearse adequately (which in turn helps me to commit to the shot)
-   be sure that I line up well, to a specific target (so as to eliminate this as a possible source of error)

This all sounds straightforward but it was far from easy to implement. It took a long time to get used to my new routine, and even now I have lapses. But when it's working I am far more efficient. I now think, choose, rehearse, setup and play my shots in one smooth flow. Plus I know that, barring lapses, I have setup and aimed well (and I mentioned before the importance of aiming correctly – I believe this should be at the core of any serious golfer's routine).

After the shot, a smart golfer also looks to capture any information that will help him assess how it went. Firstly he will look at his divot to see if that tells a story. In the case where the shot goes exactly or roughly online, and the expected distance, that is probably all he needs to do.

But if the shot was poor, or in some way unsatisfactory, our golfer will pause for a moment to consider what happened, and make a mental note of any possible reasons that come to mind. If there was an obvious problem then this becomes a prompt to make sure he gets things right on the next shot.

The smart golfer moves calmly and smoothly around the course, making everything appear 'routine'.

SMART GOLFER CHECKLIST – ROUTINE

- O   Think ahead on the way around
- O   Have a rough plan before reaching the ball
- O   Develop and commit to a pre-shot routine
- O   Routinely capture post-shot information

30.   POSITIVE ATTITUDE

A smart golfer is aware of his physical and mental state, adopts a rational and positive attitude, and seeks help when needed.

The smart golfer tries to be clear in advance of what he wants to achieve from a given round of golf. But he is also prepared to modify his aims if needed, accepting that there will be occasions when we are all physically or mentally tired.

The effects of physical tiredness are often evident. For example, you might find yourself 'dragging around' the course, or it might seem like more effort than usual to make a full swing with your driver. You might also have a problem with your posture – someone experiencing this is likely to appear less athletic over the ball, and possibly be stooping, with rounded shoulders. In this state the swing will certainly suffer.

The presence and effect of mental tiredness is less obvious. If your mind isn't working well, it is natural that you might not be aware of it! But if you ever have a bad day for no apparent reason, this could be as a result of mental tiredness. In fact in many instances this is *the main reason* for a bad round.

So the smart golfer accepts that there might be negative consequences if he is tired. In this state his decisions and choices are likely to be less good than normal, and it will be difficult to concentrate. If he screws-up, it might take also take him longer to 'deal with it'. In addition, the reduced level of focus and awareness will make it more difficult to produce a smooth swing. Often when the mind slumps, the body does too.

Whilst 'being tired' isn't a reason not to play, it is a reason to lower expectations. When I am tired, I typically say to myself: *The outcome from today isn't so important. I know that I might struggle with my swing and that my judgments won't be as good as normal. I'll just set out to have some fun with my playing partners, get enjoyment from playing some good shots here and there, and appreciate the exercise and fresh air.*

Despite feeling energetic when you start, tiredness can creep in whilst you play. During a round the smart golfer makes sure he keeps his energy and hydration levels up. Bananas and cereal bars are most popular to give an energy boost. And many golfers also make sure that they drink at least one bottle of water or cordial on the way around, whatever the weather.

After a round, asking and answering questions about your play as you arrive at the clubhouse, or later on when you return home, is one of the 'rituals of golf'. For many years when I was asked *how was it?*, I used to just ramble on, with no coherent answer. It seemed to me that many others did this too (I guess we were doing passable impressions of being 'golf bores'!). For my own part I was just trying to rationalise how I had played, but I often struggled to put this into words.

Thinking about this, I started to work out what 'good' meant to me (in terms of a round of golf). It was clear that a large part of how I felt was determined by the expectations I had before I started. Irrespective of how high or low these expectations were, if I met or exceeded them, I was generally happy. But because I am quite demanding of myself (not to mention competitive!), I was more often than not disappointed.

The smart golfer however knows that losing and winning are integral parts of playing golf.

In match play, a golfer with a representative handicap won't win much more than half the time. And for every streak of winning, there will be an equivalent one of losing (unless the handicaps are wrong). Match play also has the other factor of how well your opponent played and, if you are playing pairs, there is also the extent to which your partner contributed, or not.

In stroke play competitions, winning is even less likely. With a field of 50 players, it will be difficult to come in the top ten, let alone in the top three. But it is interesting to note that if you are an 'improving golfer' the odds go up quite significantly.

The smart golfer therefore appreciates that it is important to decouple the 'result' from the rest of the experience. After a competitive round, I try to break things down a bit. For example I might say something like:

- *I played well* (my judgement on how well I performed)
- *I didn't score as well as I played* (the extent to which my score reflected my play)
- *It was great fun* (the level of enjoyment I experienced)

The three elements (performance, score and enjoyment) are linked. But any one of them could be up, whilst the others are down, and vice versa. These days I find that the most important things to me are firstly to enjoy myself, and secondly to do the best I can on the day. Provided I don't give up, remain positive, and the company is good, then nothing else matters.

I am comforted to know that if I perform well I will on average get good results. And that from time to time despite playing well, my score, or the match outcome, will not go my way. But on other days I won't play so well and I will win my match. That's golf!

It's the same for individual shots as it is for a round of golf. There are things you can't control, like whether a critical putt drops or not. The outcome is therefore somewhat random, and to some degree contains a measure of 'luck'. To consider this further you might attempt to measure how lucky you were after a given round. Assess and rate each shot as being lucky, unlucky, or neither (to make this easier it is perhaps best to limit this exercise to just long shots only).

As you go through your shots, try to distinguish between a poor outcome that you deserved (for a bad decision or shot), and one that you didn't (where you prepared well and made a good swing). It is easy to credit yourself for a good outcome without thinking, despite the reality that many of these shots will have had a measure of luck in them.

Over time you should have as many lucky as unlucky shots unless your judgment is biased.

Many golfers repeatedly believe they have more bad luck than good, and are frustrated as a result. Yet clearly this cannot be the case. Others in a slump might also be particularly negative about their rounds and form at the present, and to some extent this is natural. But by and large these phases pass, and good golf should return.

From my experience of observing golfers over the years, I have concluded that it helps to be realistic, rational, and positive about golf. Those who adopt this attitude seem to me to be more content over the long term. There is little point in being perpetually negative. This merely shows that expectations are too high, and one obvious solution is to lower them.

The smart golfer seeks help with his game if this is needed. Throughout this book I have made quite a few references to the role that lessons can play in smartening up your game. These are there to remind readers that, no matter how much we try to help ourselves, there is a limit to how much can be achieved this way. If a golfer is really determined to improve his score, or lower his handicap, it makes sense to take a lesson here and there, provided the cost is bearable.

Many players though, have a negative attitude to seeking help of any kind. The reasons for this seem to be more emotional than rational. Some golfers have been influenced by stories of players who started lessons only to struggle with their swings for a long time afterwards. But even taking this stance should not preclude having a lesson or two to address other aspects of your game (such as chipping, bunker play and putting).

There are also a group of players who, for whatever reason, don't want *to be seen to be* taking lessons. Some smart golfers I know have solved this problem by getting lessons 'on the quiet' at another club or driving range nearby. If you think a professional might be able to help, but for whatever reason don't like the thought of taking lessons at your club, why not consider this as a possibility?

Clearly self-improvement should be the preferred way for many golfers to address shortcomings in the first instance. But from time to time we will all inevitably come up against problems that we just can't crack without help. Sometimes these can simply be resolved by asking a friend (typically a better standard golfer) to take a look at the issue. By and large, the smart golfers I know don't hesitate to get some assistance if required.

The smart golfer is aware of his physical and mental state, adopts a rational and positive attitude, and seeks help when needed.

SMART GOLFER CHECKLIST – POSITIVE ATTITUDE

- O Be wary of mental tiredness
- O Be wary of physical tiredness and poor posture
- O Adjust expectations as required
- O Top up with energy snacks, and stay hydrated
- O Separate performance, score and enjoyment (post-round)
- O Accept that over time there is no such thing as bad luck
- O Be realistic, rational and positive
- O Understand that there is a limit to self-help
- O Accept that a golf lesson may be the best answer

31.   PLAYING THE GAME

A smart golfer has integrity, shows consideration for others, and understands and adheres to the rules of the game.

Golf is one of the few sports where the rules are 'self-administered'. Primary responsibility for staying within the rules, and spotting a breach, rests with the player himself. Golfers therefore need to be aware of the rules, and to be mindful of their actions at all times.

The standards expected of golfers are set out by The R&A, the governing standards and rules body, who take their name from The Royal and Ancient Golf Club of St Andrews. The R&A is the governing body for golf played around the world with the exception of the USA and Mexico, which are the responsibility of The United States Golf Association (The USGA).

The Old Course in St Andrews is often described as 'the home of golf', and the rules can be considered to be at the very heart of the game. I show below, with the kind permission of The R&A, an extract from the Rules of Golf and The R&A's website, which gives a sense of what I mean by this:

"Golf is played, for the most part, without the supervision of a referee or umpire. The game relies on the integrity of the individual to show consideration for other players, care for the course and to abide by the Rules.

Players should conduct themselves in a disciplined manner, demonstrating courtesy and sportsmanship at all times, irrespective of how competitive they may be.

Etiquette is an integral and inextricable part of the game, which has come to define golf's values worldwide. Put simply, it is a series of guidelines that exist to show other players, whether through divot repair or awareness of your shadow, a degree of fairness that you would expect to receive in return.

In terms of golf's environment, etiquette is about showing respect for the course on which you are playing and the work that has been put in to create it.

It's about making sure that the game is played safely and that others on the course are able to enjoy the round as much as you.

In short: it is about showing consideration to all others on the course at all times."

These words illustrate that every golfer is expected to show good sportsmanship. Provided all concerned 'play the game', this behaviour can make all the difference to everyone's enjoyment on the day.

In addition to demonstrating this on the course, it is to everyone's benefit to maintain these values off it as well, for example immediately after an important match. The best exponents of

••
The extracts in this chapter from The R&A's Rules of Golf and their website are the copyright of The Royal and Ancient Golf Club of St Andrews.

good etiquette are nearly always humble in victory (despite perhaps wanting to crow about it) and magnanimous in defeat (even if inside they are feeling hard done by, perhaps because they think their opponents had more than their fair share of good fortune).

There are many examples of good sportsmanship and exemplary behaviour amongst professional golfers. A good example that neatly sums-up what this is all about is a quote from the great Ben Hogan near the end of his life. When asked how he would like to be remembered he replied: "*As a gentleman first, and next as a golfer.*"

In addition to the principles and spirit in which the game should be played, The Rules of Golf set the boundaries of what is allowed, and provide order and equity to the situations that we find ourselves in during the course of a round. There are an almost infinite variety of possibilities that could crop up so the rules are, of necessity, comprehensive. This makes them a somewhat daunting read.

Nevertheless, the smart golfer knows the rules well. As a result he is more certain of his actions and the options available to him in difficult situations. This enables him to concentrate on playing without the presence of doubt. He is also able to readily help fellow golfers in the spirit of consideration and camaraderie. In match play, knowing what to do when others don't, can also give a player a psychological advantage.

There are several ways to get up to speed with the rules. In the UK most golf clubs provide their members with a free copy of the pocket version of the rulebook. At the front of this is a section called A Quick Guide to the Rules of Golf that is essential reading for the serious player. Many golfers also keep the pocket version in their golf bags for the odd occasion when a problem crops up and it really matters.

In addition, The R&A's website is most helpful and includes an online rules 'look up' facility together with a variety of tools and apps that can help a player get up to speed or resolve a particular issue. Alternatively there are also many illustrated books that explain the rules in a straightforward manner, and that give examples of what to do in different situations.

In addition to describing what is not permitted, there are many rules that can be helpful in problem situations. I discussed several of these earlier in this book including Playing a Provisional, Searching for a Lost Ball, and Dropping Under Penalty.

Golfers also benefit from understanding other key rules (both the entitlement to relief and the procedure for gaining relief). These include Ground Under Repair, Casual Water, Animal Scrapings, Cut or Damaged Ball, Marks on the Green and Immovable and Moveable Obstructions.

In addition to the official rules, each club will have a number of 'local rules'. These will change from time to time and might cover the:
- identification and location of Water Hazards and Out of Bounds
- identification, location and procedure for Ground Under Repair
- entitlement to relief from Paths and Roads, Embedded Ball, Sprinkler Heads, Aeration Holes and Staked Trees, and
- entitlement to Clean and Place the ball, such as in winter or bad weather conditions

For a specific course, permanent local rules are typically shown on the back of the scorecard. The smart golfer makes a point of reading these before playing at a course he is unfamiliar with. Temporary local rules (such as for winter rules in season) are usually displayed in the club (for example on a noticeboard), listed near the first tee, or are advised to golfers from day to day by club staff.

All golfers will from time to time find themselves in a situation where neither they, nor their playing partners, know what to do. If it is a friendly game, then the problem is typically resolved by the majority view. But in competition, the rules specify what should be done when there is Doubt as to Procedure.

Golfers who are ignorant of the rules will from time to time fail to take advantage of something that is their right, or fall foul of something that will penalise their play.

For example, the rules relating to a Ball Moving Accidentally and a Ball Moving due to an Outside Agency are often not well understood or applied, particularly the part about replacing the ball after you are 'deemed' to have moved it yourself. It is not uncommon for players to be penalised for unknowingly breaching these rules, so it is better to be well informed in order to avoid disagreement and disappointment.

The smart golfer therefore appreciates the need to be 'up on the rules'. In doing so he is able to be more confident of his and others' actions as he plays, and is readily able to help resolve problems as they arise.

Very few golfers will cite the rules as being something they love about golf. But nearly all hardened golfers have respect for them. They realise that the rules are necessary to provide clarity and fairness. In doing so they contribute greatly to everyone's enjoyment.

The smart golfer has integrity, shows consideration for others, and understands and adheres to the rules of the game.

SMART GOLFER CHECKLIST – PLAYING THE GAME

- ○ Be 'mindful' on the golf course
- ○ Act with honesty and integrity
- ○ Be 'up to speed' on the rules
- ○ Check 'local rules' before starting a round

CONCLUSION

In this book I set out to share some of what I have learned from my experiences of golf, particularly to help others improve. I hope you found it interesting, and that in some way it leads to you being more content with your play.

I have discussed the tee, lies, slopes, distances, wind, elevation, local knowledge, handling trouble, lost balls, fairway bunkers, rough, trees, pitching, chipping, greenside bunkers and all manner of putts – quite a tour. I also emphasised that is is important to:
- think in terms of accuracy and consistency
- have a good 'routine'
- make sound decisions
- be able to analyse your problems
- prepare well before a round
- be knowledgeable on the rules; and to
- have a rational and positive attitude

In many respects the points I make throughout are simply common sense. Yet golf is such a complex game, as shown by the sheer variety of subjects and situations I have discussed. And this is without even considering 'the swing' itself.

Unlike with many other sports, each shot in golf starts and ends with a stationary ball. This presents a massive opportunity for us to use our heads to get the best possible outcome, and to more readily see and understand the mistakes that we make. Hopefully this book will provide you with a framework to achieve this yourself.

There are a whole host of reasons why we play the game. Many golfers state it is because they love the sensation of making a 'pure strike' with a driver, or the 'rush' from sinking a critical putt. Others refer to the fun of competition, or the mental and physical challenge. Yet for some it is simply the chance to get some exercise in pleasant surroundings with good company.

Nearly all also mention the positive social experience, and the camaraderie, spirit and sense of community found amongst players of all standards. Golf is a game where the vast majority of players embrace good sportsmanship, and adhere to the rules without question. This creates a shared belief system based on integrity and consideration for others. Few other sports come anywhere close to matching this.

For me it is simply the greatest game on earth.

David Richards

ABOUT THE AUTHOR AND THE BOOK

David Richards is a semi-retired business professional with a background in electronics, engineering, project management and business consultancy. He lives and plays most of his golf in Hertfordshire, where he is a member of a local club. He regularly plays different courses, particularly enjoys match play golf and captained his club side for several years.

Some time ago it became clear to David that his swing was a fundamental problem in his game and that, no matter how hard he tried, there would be a limit to what he could do about it. But he still wanted to play the best possible golf and to get his handicap down. So he set out on a mission to do this, despite the limitations of his swing.

He initially looked to books for help. But he found that whilst there were many publications on technique and 'the mind game', there was virtually nothing that helped with assessing a shot, decision-making and analysing where shots are lost.

Over several years he worked on his own game, observed others wrestling with theirs, and in particular studied golfers who always seemed to score well, even when their swing or short games were a bit off on the day. With much hard work he managed to get his handicap down. After an enjoyable period of shooting rounds in the 70s, it occurred to him that the knowledge that he had accumulated might be used to help others, in the form of a book.

His fellow golfers, including the golf professional who now helps with his swing, encouraged him to make this a reality. They pointed out that whilst he is not a professional golfer, a teaching professional, or a psychologist, in many ways he is better placed to write a book like this than they would be.

Firstly, he has an analytical mind, honed by years of designing engineering solutions and solving business problems. Secondly, he has observed thousands of rounds played by regular golfers (which is more than many teaching professionals). Thirdly, he has tried all manner of ways in which to improve his own game and discussed this widely (giving him good experience of what does, and does not, work in practice). These factors combined have enabled him to write a practical book that focuses on many of the key elements that contribute to scoring well.

In writing the book, one of David's objectives was to make it easy to read and use. The book is set out in about 30 separate chapters, each covering a different aspect of the game. At the end of each chapter there is a checklist that highlights the principles covered. This can be used either as an aide memoire or for readers to easily compare themselves to a 'smart golfer'.

David hopes that *Playing Smart* will help readers to find ways to improve their own games, and to experience the contentment that comes from being able to play to a better standard.

www.playing-smart.com